Thou Shalt Not Steal

TRANSLATED WORKS OF PIERRE VIRET:

The Christian and the Magistrate

Letters of Comfort to the Persecuted Church

No Other God: a Practical Look at a Personal God

Simple Exposition of the Christian Faith

Thou Shalt Not Kill: A Plea for Life

FURTHER TITLES AVAILABLE FROM PSALM 78 MINISTRIES

Call Me No Hero

Dangerous Endeavor: the Lewis and Clark Expedition,
From Their Journals

Driven to Resistance: A History of the Revolutionary War,
as told by those who lived it

John Paton for Young Folks

The New England Primer:
Essential Textbook of Christian Education

New Testament Greek for the Beginner

Pierre Viret: the Angel of the Reformation

Pirates, Puritans, and the Perils of the High Seas

Without a Home or Country: A Gallant Tale of the
Last Stand of the Confederate Navy

For a full listing of titles, please visit: www.psalm78ministries.com

Thou Shalt Not Steal

A call for honest dealings in business,
civil, and personal relationships

by Pierre Viret

Translated by R. A. Sheats

Psalm 78 Ministries

www.psalm78ministries.com

Thou Shalt Not Steal: A call for honest dealings in business, civil, and personal relationships

by Pierre Viret

Translated by R. A. Sheats

First printing, 2017

Published by:

Psalm 78 Ministries
P. O. Box 950
Monticello, FL 32345

www.psalm78ministries.com

ISBN: 978-1-938822-59-9

Printed in the United States of America.

Biblical quotations are taken from the King James Version of the Holy Scriptures. Divine pronouns have been capitalized.

TABLE OF CONTENTS

Translator's Note

Thou Shalt Not Steal is an English translation of a portion of Viret's commentary on the Ten Commandments, published originally in 1564 in French under the title *Instruction Chrestienne en la doctrine de la loy et de l'Evangile,* and printed in Geneva by Jean Rivery. With the intention of presenting his readers with an easily-understood, down-to-earth exposition of the Ten Commandments, Viret wrote his commentary as a conversation between two fictitious characters, Daniel and Timothy. *Thou Shalt Not Steal* enters the conversation as Timothy and Daniel begin to discuss the meaning and application of the eighth commandment.

Unless otherwise noted, Scripture quotations are taken from the King James Version of the Holy Bible. Chapter breaks and headings have been added for ease of comprehension and do not appear in the original. Footnotes and Scripture references in brackets have also been added for clarification and do not appear in the original French text.

CHAPTER ONE

Keeping the Eighth Commandment

"Thou shalt not steal."
— Exodus 20:15

THE PURPOSE OF THE EIGHTH COMMANDMENT, AND HOW IT IS TO BE FULFILLED IN ITS ENTIRETY

TIMOTHY: You said that, when it pleased me, you were ready to explain to me the eighth commandment, which God gave against theft; but it is not for me, who I consider no more than your disciple, to choose the time that suits me, but to you, whom I take as my teacher.

DANIEL: If it is proper for the disciple to submit himself to the good pleasure of his master in the manner that you say, it is no less necessary for the master to accommodate himself to his disciple and to all the means which he considers to be the most proper for his benefit. Therefore, seeing that I perceive you are prepared to listen and understand, I am also ready to pursue the object you desire.

TIMOTHY: There are already certain points which are easy for me to understand because of what you have said concerning the other commandments.

The first is that, as the Lord willed by the two preceding commandments to provide for the preservation of human life and of man's body, and for both his own purity and honesty as well as that of those persons joined to him, He here in a similar way gives a law for the preservation of the goods given man by God for the necessities of this life, and of the houses and families raised and constructed by means of marriage.

Secondly, when He said "Thou shalt not steal," I understand that by this prohibition He both forbids us to steal and also commands us to do the contrary. Thus I conclude that God not only here forbids me from doing any harm in any way whatever to the goods of my neighbor, but that He also commands me, first, to labor by all means possible to preserve and increase his goods and, second, to assist and aid him with my own goods in his time of need. If I do not do this, I do not fulfill this commandment as God requires of me.

THE LOVE AND GENEROSITY REQUIRED FOR THE OBSERVANCE OF THIS COMMANDMENT; AND THE COVETOUSNESS AND GREED FORBIDDEN BY IT; AND HOW IT IS NECESSARY TO BE POOR IN SPIRIT TO FULFILL IT; AND WHO MUST BE CONSIDERED AS SUCH

DANIEL: You conclude very well, for we must not doubt that if the love and generosity God requires of us toward our neighbors does not exist in us as it ought to, their counterpart, which is greed, will surely dwell in their place. And greed cannot exist without coveting the goods of others. Therefore, by condemning the fruit which it produces, this commandment admonishes us to uproot this wicked root (1 Tim. 6:10-11). For, seeing that "the law is spiritual" and the Lawgiver is spiritual as well, we must always proceed to its spiritual fulfillment and to the reformation of heart from which this work proceeds (Rom. 7:14). For, as Jesus Christ testified: "evil thoughts, murders, adulteries, fornications, thefts, false witness, [and] blasphemies" all proceed "out of the heart" (Mat. 15:19). Thus, if we wish to fulfill this commandment, it is necessary for us to truly be of the number of these "poor in spirit" whom Jesus Christ calls "blessed," and to whom He promises "the kingdom of heaven" (Mat. 5:3; Luke 6:20).

TIMOTHY: Who are they who must be taken for such people?

DANIEL: Those who are truly known to be such people are fully humbled in their heart, placing no confidence either in themselves or their riches or any creature at all, but only in God alone and in His riches (Jer. 9:23-24). For what is the source of our covetousness and greed except the absence of the knowledge of the poverty which exists in us and the riches that we possess in God, and the means of obtaining them and of enjoying the use of them? This ignorance is truly the reason why we mistrust God, just as this unbelief is the cause of the confidence that we place in ourselves, which we would not place there if we didn't doubt God. And we would not distrust Him if we truly recognized that we cannot ever obtain any goods at all except from His hand. For, for lack of this knowledge, we seek in ourselves what we ought to await from Him; and we seek it not by the means that He has ordained, but by those means which seem better and more fitting to us.

Therefore, until we have learned with Paul to be rich and to be poor (as he wrote of himself to the Philippians) and "to abound" and "to suffer need," we cannot ever fulfill this commandment in its entirety (Phil. 4:11-12). For, firstly, if we cannot endure any poverty, and if we do not know how to find consolation in it, we could not restrain ourselves from taking to ourselves the goods of another by unlawful means. And therefore this lesson of Paul's is more than necessary for us, in order that we might learn to conform ourselves to the good will of God and to content ourselves with what He has already given and bestowed on us, be it little or much.

TIMOTHY: It seems to me that it is much easier to be content with much than with little. For poverty and need are very harsh and fierce masters, who often constrain many people—indeed, even honest men—to do very dishonest things.

DANIEL: I agree that these masters are very difficult to bear with, but truly they can never gain any victory over an honest and God-fearing man (or one who has learned Paul's lesson you just heard) in such a way that they force him to commit a dishonest act. But if the person does not possess such a fear of God as he ought, poverty and need will not make him wicked; they will only reveal the wickedness that was already in his heart, though it was hidden and covered until an occasion offered itself to reveal it.

And, concerning your statement that it seemed much easier to be content with much than with little, I am truly of an opinion quite contrary to yours. For it is much more difficult for rich men to be content than for poor men. For, instead of a poor man who contents himself with very little, rich men are always bottomless pits who can never be content with anything. Therefore they always want to have all, without leaving anything for the poor. This cruelty is always joined with greed, which renders them more inhuman than savage beasts, so much so that, if they were able to staunch and dry up the waters to get rid of the poor, they would do so. Or, if they could gather all the waters together in such a way that they could keep it all for themselves, they would do it. They would do no less with the sun (as Chrysostom once reproached them), if they were able to deprive the poor people of its light and brightness. And therefore it is not without reason that Paul calls it a very lofty knowledge which knows how to be content in abundance and in poverty.

HOW MEN'S DISTRUST OF GOD IS THE MAIN REASON FOR THE BREAKING OF THIS COMMANDMENT; AND TRUST IN HIS PROVIDENCE IS THE TRUE MEANS OF FULFILLING IT

TIMOTHY: It seems to me that you have discovered the root of this evil disease and have sounded its depths to the bottom. For, if we have such trust in God as we ought, we would never fear poverty and need. If this fear were removed from us, we would never be afraid, firstly, of becoming poor and falling into need by giving alms and assistance to our brothers of the goods that we have been given of God, and we would never be induced to steal the goods of others, taking it as assured that what we have received from Him will not leave us if we employ it according to His will. For, seeing that He is the Treasurer, He will always distribute to us as much as He knows to be necessary both for our own needs as well as for those of others, as He promised us by Solomon, saying: "Treasures of wickedness profit nothing: but righteousness delivereth from death. The LORD will not suffer the soul of the righteous to famish: but He casteth away the substance of the wicked" (Prov. 10:2-3). Therefore each of us has good reason to content ourselves with what it has pleased God to give us.

Secondly, after this fear and distrust is removed and we fully resign ourselves to the good will of God, we would prefer death rather than choose wicked means that He has forbidden in an attempt to relieve ourselves from this poverty and distress and enrich ourselves. Therefore we must beware of becoming thieves.

And if it happens that our goods are removed (in whatever way they might be), we should receive this as from the hand of God, and say with Job: "the LORD gave, and the LORD hath taken away; blessed be the name of the LORD" (Job 1:21).

And thirdly, this same trust will also teach us to use our abundance as it should be used, without making a god of our riches, as rich men generally do.

DANIEL: This is why Paul called them "idolaters," and called covetousness "idolatry" (Eph. 5:5; Col. 3:5).

TIMOTHY: They are idolaters of very evil gods indeed. For there are generally no men more fearful, nor who tremble more out of fear, than the rich, because of the fear they have of losing their gods.

DANIEL: This is no surprise. For, seeing that these are gods which thieves can steal, and seeing that robbers are often much stronger and more powerful than them, it happens that these gods must be guarded by those whom they ought to guard.

TIMOTHY: And therefore if the rich had learned to trust in the living and true God who can guard and nourish them, they would have more assurance than they have ever experienced before. But they can never do this while their confidence is founded on another god.

CHAPTER TWO

Thefts, Thieves, and Stealing

IN WHAT SENSE THE WORDS "STEAL," "THEFT," AND "THIEF" MUST BE UNDERSTOOD FOR THE PROPER UNDERSTANDING OF THIS COMMANDMENT ACCORDING TO THE USAGE OF THE HOLY SCRIPTURES

DANIEL: You speak very well, by which I perceive that you have not poorly understood what I have explained. Therefore, from what I can see, you will soon have no great need of being taught by me, for you already know enough to be a teacher as well as a disciple.

TIMOTHY: You would truly have wasted your time in teaching me if my understanding were not a little more enlightened now than it was at the beginning, after hearing you for such a long time, and if I had not profited in some way within your school. But yet I always find many things to learn from you.

We have spoken until now of the primary foundation of the fulfillment and transgression of this commandment. Now let us proceed to the rest.

DANIEL: We must first observe what these words *steal, theft,* and *thief* mean, and then we will speak of the various types of thefts and the manners by which they are committed.

TIMOTHY: This is just what I ask. Thus tell me first of all what you understand by the word *steal.*

DANIEL: The Hebrew word which Moses uses in this

commandment properly means "to take by stealth," "to remove," or "to take and remove something secretly, without the knowledge of those who possess it." Laban used it in this sense when he said to Jacob, "You have robbed me of my heart"—that is, "thou hast stolen away unawares to me" (Gen. 31:26). When he said, "thou hast stolen away unawares," he explains what he said previously: "you have robbed me of my heart," and what the Scripture said also, that "Jacob stole away unawares to Laban the Syrian"—that is, "he stole away secretly" with his family and "he told him not that he had fled," and did not let Laban his father-in-law know (Gen. 31:20).

And Joseph said: "I was stolen away out of the land of the Hebrews" because he had been taken by his brothers without his father's knowledge (Gen. 40:15).

It is also written of Absalom that he "stole the hearts of the men of Israel," which is the same as saying that he deceived, attracted, and seduced them secretly after himself (2 Sam. 15:6). And in this same place the Israelites said to David: "Why have our brethren the men of Judah stolen thee away?" because the line of Judah single-handedly brought him back to his house without the knowledge of the other Israelites and without having called for their assistance (2 Sam. 19:41). It is also said of the people: "the people gat them by stealth that day into the city," which means that they entered *secretly*, as if they *stole into* the city (2 Sam. 19:4). Thus this word, taken according to the usage in the Holy Scriptures, does not only mean "to take the possessions of one's neighbor without their knowledge," but also "to mislead and deceive with cunning," however it might be done.

THE DIFFERENCE BETWEEN HUMAN AND DIVINE LAWS CONCERNING STEALING; AND THE REASON WHY GOD USED THE WORD "STEAL" IN THIS COMMANDMENT

TIMOTHY: Do other laws use the word in this way?

DANIEL: According to the common definition, we define *theft* as the usurpation of the possessions of another without the consent or knowledge of the one to whom they belong. According to this definition, greed, miserliness, a lack of generosity and charity, covetousness of the heart, or many other types of harm by which our neighbor is harmed either in his own person or in a lack of assistance and aid which is due him by the duty of Christian charity, are not properly understood as theft. Therefore we must here consider that the Law of God looks much deeper than human laws, as we have already said repeatedly. And yet this word *theft* bears a much wider definition when we consider it theologically (which is divine and spiritual knowledge) than according to civil laws. Thus it is not enough if we simply avoid the name of *thief* among men and in the eyes of civil justice, unless we are also absolved of this crime by the Law of God.

And because these names of *theft* and *thief* are so odious, dishonorable, and despicable among men, the Lord willed to comprehend by them all the sins that He desires to forbid by this commandment, in order that we might not hold anything in as great abomination as we do this crime which men call *theft*. And then He also shows us the greatest sins by the least, for if He is displeased when we retain the possessions of our neighbor without his knowledge, then He certainly cannot approve of those who retain them with their knowledge, by force and violence, as do robbers and highwaymen.

HOW THE NAMES "THEFT" AND "THIEF" ARE HELD IN GREATER DETESTATION AMONG MEN THAN THE ACT OF THEFT; AND HOW THOSE WHO DO NOT MEET THE NEEDS OF THEIR NEIGHBORS WHEN IT IS IN THEIR POWER TO DO SO ARE THIEVES

TIMOTHY: Therefore He uses these words, aiming at the same end, according to the nature of the sins He regards, which we already spoke of on murder and adultery. But there are few people who understand this and who think about it.

It is certain that the word *theft* is so vile among men that there is scarcely any insult greater than to be called a thief. Therefore if we would hold this crime in as great an abhorrence as we do its name, we would be much more afraid of falling into this sin than we are now; and we would not consider miserliness, covetousness, and greed to be such little things, nor many other types of actions by which we either harm our neighbors or abandon them without helping them.

DANIEL: This is doubtless true. For we would find it very strange if someone called us thieves every time we didn't give alms to those who were in need when we had the means to do so. Yet this is exactly how the matter stands before God in truth. How then ought we to consider those who not only deny assistance to their brethren when they are in need, but what is even worse, who harm them instead of assisting them?

TIMOTHY: What you say agrees well with the reproach Jesus Christ made to the wicked and reprobates and with the praise that He gave to the faithful and elect in the form of His judgment to come which is set forth for us by Matthew. He did not reproach them for pillaging or stealing, but reproached them for the contempt they had shown to His poor members by not aiding them at all when they ought to have done so, just as He praised the others for doing the contrary (Mat. 25:31-46).

DANIEL: There is a very clear reason for this. For, seeing that all the possessions we have are given to us by God not only for us, but also to share with our brothers according to the rule of love which He gave to us, we cannot deny that we are thieves when we withhold from our brothers what has been delivered to us to share with them. For by doing this we keep for ourselves what belongs to another just as much as if the servant of a ruler kept for himself the money which was placed in his hands to be delivered to the poor. For this reason, though we do not read that the rich man to whom Jesus Christ speaks in the Gospel according to Luke had pillaged, robbed, or shown violence to Lazarus either in his person or his possessions, yet he still did not escape God's condemnation because he was not loving, merciful, and generous toward that poor beggar full of sores who lay begging at his gate (Luke 16:19-25).

HOW GOD DIVIDES HIS BLESSINGS AMONG MEN, AND THE THEFT COMMITTED BY THEM, AND HOW GOD'S ORDER IS CONFOUNDED AMONG MEN BY THIS

TIMOTHY: If he is a thief who withholds what has been given him to bestow on others, how then ought we to regard the man who not only does this but, what is even worse, takes what belongs to others, which was given them by God both for their own use and to bestow upon their other brethren?

DANIEL: You can easily judge this by what you have just heard. Thus for us to properly guard ourselves from this sin, we must firstly recognize it as something absolutely certain that every man has the possessions which he has by the order and provision of God, who as a wise Father divides His goods among His children as He pleases. Therefore Job recognized that he had received from Him all that he possessed in this world (Job 1:21; 2:10). You also heard what we said on the fifth commandment concerning the division of the earth that God made to the inhabitants of it, which we must also understand of all the possessions which are on it.

Therefore we must each content ourselves with the portion that He has given us, without laying our hands on that of others, and without coveting in our heart. For if we do otherwise, we set ourselves against the commandment of our Father, and He will not receive us when we destroy and confound the order which He has placed among men regarding the use of His creation.

So also we must beware of misusing what we have already been given, but instead we must faithfully employ it in the uses for which He gave it to us, as stewards who will give an account to Him of what He placed in our hands to be given out.

CHAPTER THREE

Christian Communion versus Communism

THE COMMANDMENT GOD MADE CONCERNING THE OWNERSHIP AND SHARING OF EARTHLY POSSESSIONS, AND THE THINGS NECESSARY FOR ITS PRESERVATION—THAT IS, CONTRACTS AND POLITICAL LAWS TO UPHOLD JUSTICE AMONG MEN

TIMOTHY: From what I can see, this commandment is wholly contrary to the confused sharing of possessions that some wild spirits—seditious madmen—have labored to implement, and particularly certain Anabaptists who have arisen in our time, who desire that nothing be owned by any particular person in order that rascals and mischief-makers might by this means make a vast spoil of the possessions of the rich who were deceived by them under the name and title of charity, as was previously done by the priests and monks under the guise of purchasing the salvation of their souls.

DANIEL: The matter is very clear, for we here see quite openly that God, by forbidding theft, commanded a distinction both of owners and of possessions, and that He established a particular ownership of things among men, and consequently that He gave a command concerning the contracts which are necessary among men to maintain and preserve life and human society.

For, firstly, if nothing belonged to anyone in particular and if no one could say "That's mine" or "That's yours," there could never be any theft, seeing that theft cannot exist unless something that belongs to someone is taken and stolen. For, if all possessions were held in common, no one could ever take anything that belonged to someone else.

Also, seeing that everyone must know that all that belongs to him has been given to him by God and that there is no one who possesses all that is necessary for himself in such a way that he is self-sufficient without in any way being assisted by others and by what God has given them, it is necessary firstly that there be some manner of communion by which some assist others and provide for needs which may exist.

Secondly, in order to preserve proper order in this communion and to remove disorder and confusion (for which God ordained the private ownership which exists among earthly things), it is necessary to have forms of contracts, ruled by good laws and administrations of justice, in order that there be no injury, damage, violence, or deceit by anyone in this communion and in the use of these possessions. By this we clearly see how this law given against theft is a foundation and a command of all these things and of all good civil laws and honest administrations of justice which serve for the public peace of human life and the equity which is required in it.

TIMOTHY: What you say is quite evident, but all do not consider these things as deeply as you do.

HOW THIS COMMANDMENT CANNOT BE FULFILLED UNLESS THE HEART IS PURGED OF ALL COVETOUSNESS AND ALL CONFIDENCE IN RICHES, AND UNLESS IT IS FULL OF TRUE LOVE

DANIEL: Now you must understand that all that I have said cannot be accomplished as it ought to be unless the heart is purged of all covetousness and greed, and unless it is firstly disposed to all love and generosity, as we have already said. For, as Jesus Christ said on this point: "No man can serve two masters," that is, "Ye cannot serve God and mammon" (Mat. 6:24; Luke 16:13). Therefore He commands: "Make to yourselves friends of the mammon of unrighteousness; that . . . they may receive you into everlasting habitations" (Luke 16:9). These riches are unrighteous as long as they are not employed as they ought to be, and are for us an occasion of being found unrighteous before God and our neighbors when we set our hearts on them. For this reason He also admonishes us to "lay up for yourselves treasures in heaven, where neither moth nor rust doth corrupt, and where thieves do not break through nor steal," and where they will be secure from all risk, and "provide yourselves bags which wax not old, a treasure in the heavens that faileth not, where no thief approacheth, neither moth corrupteth" (Mat. 6:20; Luke 12:33).

Likewise the psalmist says to this same purpose: "if riches increase, set not your heart upon them" (Ps. 62:10). And Paul, following this, warns the rich to "be not highminded, nor trust in uncertain riches, but in the living God, who giveth us richly all things to enjoy." Thus, they ought to be generous and charitable and ready to give and to bestow their riches on others, as he himself declares (1 Tim. 6:17-18; 2 Cor. 9:11).

He also shows them the danger in which greed places men when he says that "they that will be rich fall into temptation and a snare, and into many foolish and hurtful lusts, which drown men in destruction and perdition" (1 Tim. 6:9). Therefore our Lord Jesus, because of the great difficultly of properly employing riches without setting one's heart upon them, did not say without cause that "it is easier for a camel to go through the eye of a needle, than for a rich man to enter into the kingdom of God" (Mat. 19:24). For it is impossible to possess them without setting our heart upon them and without misusing them unless God gives us the grace and wisdom to use them as He requires. This is indeed impossible for men, but it is truly quite simple for God, just as Jesus Christ declared.

HOW THE UNIVERSAL COMMUNION OF EARTHLY POSSESSIONS REMOVES ALL USE AND EXERCISE OF LOVE AMONG MEN AS WELL AS THE COMMUNION THAT GOD REQUIRES BY IT; AND HOW IT TRANSFORMS HUMAN SOCIETY INTO A DEN OF THIEVES

TIMOTHY: There is much to think about in what you say. In this I consider that if this universal communion of the Anabaptists (and others like them) enjoyed a place among men, love and charity would no longer exist, for no one could of himself render a service to anyone else if all things were held in common. Therefore unity and friendship could not here be maintained in so great a way among men as it exists and is maintained in this loving communion of which we spoke. We have an example of this in what existed among the first Christians in Jerusalem in the early Church, which in no way contradicts what you said of the private possession of property. For it did not abolish this, but to the contrary it confirmed it, as Peter's words to Ananias clearly prove (Acts 2:44-45; 5:1-4).

DANIEL: But what is even more, instead of the love which the communion commanded by God bears with it, the other would open a door to a horrible lawlessness among men. For, if there were no laws and statutes among them to regulate and moderate the use of those things which they daily use, what would become of human life, seeing that there is still no rule, law, boundary, or punishment which can restrain man's insatiable and unbridled covetousness and contain them within the limits of reason and justice? If man had remained in the state of innocence in which he was created at the beginning, he would have no need of such a law. But, seeing that the corruption is such as it is, this order and law is so necessary for him that he cannot be a man without it, but instead he would devolve into a savage beast.

TIMOTHY: No one is able to contradict this.

THE PENALTIES AND PUNISHMENTS ORDAINED BY GOD AGAINST THE TRANSGRESSORS OF THIS COMMANDMENT, FOR THE PRESERVATION OF THE ORDER WHICH GOD HAS PLACED IN HUMAN LIFE AND SOCIETY

DANIEL: Moreover we must note on this, since God has so ordained it, that He has also ordained rewards to those who conduct themselves according to this rule, just as He promises by His blessings and promises. He has also ordained grievous penalties against the transgressors of this law, not only to be executed by men according to ordinary justice, but also by horrible vengeances which He Himself carries out daily in various ways. Therefore He said: "Woe to thee that spoilest, and thou wast not spoiled; and dealest treacherously, and they dealt not treacherously with thee! when thou shalt cease to spoil, thou shalt be spoiled; and when thou shalt make an end to deal treacherously, they shall deal treacherously with thee" (Isa. 33:1). On this we must note that the prophet did not address himself in this passage to petty thieves and robbers, but to great emperors, kings, and rulers, and to the most powerful and fearful tyrants in all the earth.

Though there might be no person in the world who would even dare to think of bringing a suit against such tyrants (but to the contrary they bring a suit against the others), yet God has truly dared to do it and to pronounce and execute the sentence against them, as He does ordinarily by means which He knows very well how to employ when it pleases Him. For He even makes His enemies themselves serve Him against His enemies. For, besides the eternal punishment which is prepared for all such persons (as it is for all other wicked people), God does not always wait until this final accounting, but instead very often punishes them with physical and temporal—and very grievous—punishments.

And, if He does not punish them by strangers, He often punishes them by the calamitous destruction of the very treasures and plunder they so wickedly obtained. Therefore the Lord said again in Deuteronomy: "But thou shalt have a perfect and just weight, a perfect and just measure shalt thou have: that thy days may be lengthened in the land" (Deut. 25:15). He declares by this that God often punishes those who do the contrary with death and grievous torments. And Solomon writes: "An inheritance may be gotten hastily at the beginning; but the end thereof shall not be blessed" (Prov. 20:21).

TIMOTHY: Experience proves what you say, which has given rise to the common proverb among men: "Ill-gotten gains will have an evil end." And again: "An inheritance gained by wickedness will not be enjoyed by the third generation."

DANIEL: Though experience daily convinces us of it and bears evident witness to the fact that the Word of God and His commandments are not void, yet we do not believe what we see with our own eyes and touch with our own hands, and we do not believe Him enough to restrain ourselves from working harm to our neighbors and brethren.

TIMOTHY: You speak the truth. For we are so blind that we do not know how to perceive what we are seeing or how to judge as we ought.

DANIEL: Therefore let us heed what the Lord said: "Whoso is partner with a thief hateth his own soul" (Prov. 29:24), and consider that Paul placed thieves among those who will be excluded from the kingdom of God (1 Cor. 6:9). Thus let us practice what is commanded us elsewhere: "Thou shalt not defraud thy neighbour, neither rob him" (Lev. 19:13).

TIMOTHY: This is indeed the very best counsel we could ever follow.

CHAPTER FOUR

Misers and Spendthrifts

THE TESTIMONY THAT GOD GIVES US OF HIS CHARACTER AND JUSTICE IN THIS COMMANDMENT, AS WELL AS OF HIS PROVIDENCE IN THE PRESERVATION OF OUR GOODS AND POSSESSIONS, AND THE POLITICAL ORDER AND JUSTICE WHICH HE REQUIRES AMONG MEN

DANIEL: Thus, when we hear the voice of God which declares this commandment to us, as well as the promises and threatenings joined to it, we must first take heed to the testimony which God gives us of His character and righteousness by this. For, because He is just, it is impossible for Him to be anything but a lover of justice, which cannot be justice without a true equity and fairness which, without regard for any person, equally upholds the rights of every one; as is done by means of the contracts and honest dealings which men engage in among themselves by the commandment of the Lord. For there is good reason, if I desire to have some assistance from others in what God has given them, that I also declare on my part in what way I will be able to repay the goods that I have received by what was also given to me as my portion. Therefore we make various contracts with one another in order to preserve the rights of each man.

Secondly, we must also note that God by this same means insures our goods, houses, and possessions much better than if they were enclosed and protected in high-walled and thick forts and vast fortresses; and that He also approves of the political order concerning the distinctions of goods and possessions, and that He is their Preserver. Therefore we are assured that those who in this way do us a harm or injury will not remain unpunished, and that nothing will happen to our goods any more than to our bodies and lives (for which they are given us), except as it is pleasing to Him.

Therefore let us thank Him firstly for the fatherly care which He has for us.

Secondly, if it happens that the goods which He gave us are taken from us by some unpleasant happening just as they were taken from Job, let us respond as he did, receiving this as from the hand of the Lord.

Thirdly, because we see that God approves of public order and that He loves justice and equity among us, let us beware of coveting or of taking to ourselves the goods of another by some wicked means. But let us endeavor (as much as we are able) to conform ourselves to the example of the Lord which He gave us in this commandment, and to what He requires of us in it.

THE DIFFICULTY IN SETTING FORTH THE VARIOUS TYPES OF THEFT; AND THE VICE OF WASTEFUL EXTRAVAGANCE FORBIDDEN IN THIS COMMANDMENT

TIMOTHY: Seeing that you have declared the purpose to which this commandment points and what foundation it stands upon—that is, the private ownership and possession of things, and the contracts made among men for the sharing and use of goods—tell me now the various types of theft, or at least the most common types, in order that we might better understand how we can guard against them.

DANIEL: You must not ask me to do anything more than that, for it would be impossible not only to simply declare all the types, but even the half of them. For, besides the fact that they are already innumerable, men are still daily contriving and forging new methods of theft in such a way that the thieves who were previously held in great detestation would now be considered upright and decent people in comparison with many of those who are today counted among the number of the most respectable people. But before we enter into this matter, I would like to inform you of two further points.

The first is that, as God forbade and condemned

covetousness and avarice in this commandment, commanding us instead to love and generosity, so also He forbade wastefulness, the vice which is the opposite of greed on one side and is likewise the opposite of generosity on the other side. Generosity is a virtue contrary to both the other two, though wastefulness often disguises itself under the guise of generosity (Luke 12:16-21).

We must also at the same time understand that He commands us to frugality (the virtue contrary to wastefulness), which means a moderate and reasonable use without excess on either one side or the other, which we must exercise in the disposal of the things which have been given us by God.

THE DIFFERENCE BETWEEN MISERLINESS, EXTRAVAGANCE, GENEROSITY, AND GOOD MANAGEMENT; AND HOW EXTRAVAGANT OR WASTEFUL MEN SIN AGAINST THIS COMMANDMENT IN THEIR OWN WAY JUST AS MISERLY AND GREEDY MEN DO IN THEIRS

TIMOTHY: You wish to say then that we must find a path between miserliness and wasteful extravagance.

DANIEL: It is true. For, just as miserliness passes beyond measure by hoarding what it ought not to save, so also on the opposite extreme extravagant wastefulness exceeds it on the other side by spending without concerning itself with either what or how. But the generous and moderate man and the good manager takes the moderate course in both of them, giving when he ought to give and refraining when he ought to refrain.

Now, as much as neither the miser nor the irresponsible squanderer knows how to preserve this rule and measure, they cannot avoid falling into greediness, which is one of the main sources of theft, and consequently into the other various types of it. For miserliness proceeds from this same root of distrust of God from which greed proceeds. Therefore the miser, always fearing poverty and indigence, is driven by this mistrust either to retain what he has in his hands and to make a miserly and wicked distribution among those over whom he has charge, or to steal from others to provide for himself, as the greedy man does, to relieve and comfort himself in this fear of his instead of placing his trust in God.

The irresponsible squanderer does no less in his own way, though he follows a different path. For, because he has neither bottom nor measure, he cannot be satisfied with what he ought to be, seeing that he cannot and does not know how to profitably employ what he has already foolishly squandered. Thus he must also steal something from others in order to finance his wasteful extravagance.

HOW THE IRRESPONSIBLE SQUANDERER IS A THIEF BOTH TOWARD THOSE OF HIS OWN HOUSEHOLD AS WELL AS TOWARD OTHERS

TIMOTHY: Thus he cannot fail to be a thief in many ways.

DANIEL: It cannot be otherwise. For if he has a wife and children and he leaves them to go hungry because he has foolishly spent all, he does the same as the miser who, because of his miserliness, does not provide for them the things which are necessary. Though the irresponsible squanderer proceeds in another way, yet even so the action always yields the same result.

And if by lack of his forethought his wife and daughters, constrained by poverty, surrender themselves to prostitution or debauchery, it is he himself who has sold them into this trade. And if his children give themselves up to thievery and murder or some other crimes by which they end their days on the scaffold, he himself is their executioner. Thus he is a thief because he robs them of what belongs to them and what he has been entrusted with. He was not given this to spend it in taverns or in gluttony and drunkenness and games or pomp and luxurious clothes and excess (which he might well have passed by), but in distributing it according to the needs of those who have been entrusted to him by God. Likewise, if he cannot repay those to whom he is indebted because of his wastefulness, he is also a thief by withholding the goods of others, seeing that their lack comes from his sin.

One further point is that when such persons have consumed all they own, they must come to the place when they have nothing further to eat, and must beg or borrow from someone else, though they never pay it back. Therefore it happens that they become thieves and either deceive their neighbors or steal from them by force if no one will give them anything.

HOW THE GREEDY, MISERLY, AND SPENDTHRIFTS CAN NEVER BE SATISFIED

TIMOTHY: There are many then who, when they see that they have reached the end of their resources and do not know where to draw from (as so often happens), become like desperate men as though they had lost their minds. For, by always taking out and never putting back in, an entire ocean can be exhausted; and for you to empty one hand and take from another man's to fill your other hand, is theft (1 Tim. 6:9-10).

Therefore when all is said and done, the greedy, miserly, and spendthrift are all three like a broached cask which can never be full. For, though the miser and greedy man do not scatter their wealth like the wasteful spendthrift does, yet, seeing that they never have enough and are never satisfied, what they do have is no better to them than what they do not have. Therefore their cask is no less broached and empty, when we consider it according to their desires and the use which they make of their riches, than that of the spendthrift. And they are no less dangerous, but (if I dare say it) they are more dangerous, inasmuch as no one receives any enjoyment from what they possess, as at least one does from the goods of the spendthrift (though, when all has been truly weighed and considered, there is no great difference between them).

DANIEL: The one has no tomorrow, and the others have too many. The one lives as if he only had one day to live and as if everything would perish on the morrow, and as if he desired to spend everything so that nothing might remain which was not consumed. The others live as though they would never die and as if the earth would never yield them any more fruits, but instead as though they had obtained all their provisions in one season for all eternity, and that it could never suffice for such a long time.

CHAPTER FIVE

Laziness, Labor, and Begging

THE SLOTH AND NEGLIGENCE FORBIDDEN IN THIS COMMANDMENT, AND THE VIRTUES CONTRARY TO THEM COMMENDED IN IT; AND THE LABOR COMMANDED TO MAN; AND HOW LAZINESS GIVES BIRTH TO POVERTY, AND HOW POVERTY LEADS TO THEFT AND MANY GREAT EVILS

TIMOTHY: It happens just as you say. But what is the other point that you desired to set forth after this one, as you already said?

DANIEL: It is the vices of laziness, negligence, and idleness, and the virtues of diligence, care, and labor, which are virtues opposed to these vices, which we are likewise commended and charged to uphold in this commandment just as the vices contrary to it are here condemned and forbidden. For, as we have already discussed in the commandment regarding the Sabbath, seeing that God charged man to eat bread by the sweat of his brow, it is quite certain that if man takes any other means of acquiring it, he is a thief who eats someone else's bread and not his own (Gen. 3:19). For the bread cannot be his unless it was given to him by God by the means which He has ordained (1 Cor. 4:7).

Therefore it is fitting for us to diligently consider Paul's admonition to the Thessalonians: "For yourselves know how ye ought to follow us: for we behaved not ourselves disorderly among you; neither did we eat any man's bread for nought; but wrought with labour and travail night and day, that we might not be chargeable to any of you: not because we have not power, but to make ourselves an ensample unto you to follow us. For even when we were with you, this we commanded you, that if any would not work, neither should he eat" (2 Thess. 3:7-10).

Therefore the wise man rightly sends the lazy and slothful man to the ant, to consider her ways and to learn proper economy from her. For she does not rest in times and seasons suitable for labor, but instead she "provideth her meat in the summer, and gathereth her food in the harvest," so that she might have something to eat in winter when she cannot gather the fruits of the ground (Prov. 6:6-8).

Whoever will not follow this instruction must indeed be prepared for the threat which Solomon makes in this same place to the lazy man, saying: "How long wilt thou sleep, O sluggard? when wilt thou arise out of thy sleep? Yet a little sleep, a little slumber, a little folding of the hands to sleep: so shall thy poverty come as one that travelleth, and thy want as an armed man" (Prov. 6:9-11). For, as he says in another place: "He becometh poor that dealeth with a slack hand: but the hand of the diligent maketh rich. He that gathereth in summer is a wise son: but he that sleepeth in harvest is a son that causeth shame" (Prov. 10:4-5).

Now, just as indigence and poverty proceed from negligence and laziness, so also poverty often leads men to theft and other wicked works, just as Solomon clearly shows when he made this request of God: "Two things have I required of Thee; deny me them not before I die: remove far from me vanity and lies: give me neither poverty nor riches; feed me with food convenient for me: lest I be full, and deny Thee, and say, Who is the LORD? or lest I be poor, and steal, and take the name of my God in vain" (Prov. 30:7-9).

He here asks to be delivered from two things which greatly hinder the fulfillment of this commandment:

The first is a too great abundance, which prevents us from having true poverty of spirit in such a way as we discussed earlier. For, as Jesus Christ testifies: "No man can serve two masters; . . . Ye cannot serve God and mammon" (Mat. 6:24).

The other is poverty, which often leads the poor to steal, lie, break their word, and a thousand other wickednesses. And therefore Jesus Christ taught us to ask for our daily bread from God our Father, to assure us that He will not forget to feed us (seeing that we are His children), and to warn us from going to the devil to seek our bread by wicked means when we ought to await it from the hand of God our Father.

HOW THE LAZY, INDOLENT, NEGLIGENT, IDLE, AND TRAMPS AND BEGGARS ARE THIEVES, AND MORE BEASTLY THAN SAVAGE BEASTS; AND THE REASON WHY THEY ARE DESPISED

TIMOTHY: If men would consider this well, and if they were as industrious as the ants, there would not be so many unmanly loafers, idlers, and lazy sluggards as there are on the earth; nor consequently so many tramps and beggars who drive both themselves and their wives and children to begging by their idleness, negligence, and laziness. But even worse than this are those who, not content with doing nothing and earning nothing, go even further than this by spending all their days in games and taverns. Or if they earn a dollar they spend two, and while they spend their time in drunkenness they leave their wives and children to starve at home.

DANIEL: I don't know whether these men are sane or not, or whether they are men or beasts. Paul said that: "if any provide not for his own, and specially for those of his own house, he . . . is worse than an infidel" (1 Tim. 5:8). But they are even worse than savage beasts, for even beasts care for their own—which these men do not. And what is even worse, they cannot fail to turn into thieves and to make their own family thieves in one way or another (Gen. 30:29-43). For, seeing that they do not employ themselves in any necessary work to earn the bread needful for them and their families, they will be constrained in the end to put their hand forth to labor either by theft and, if need be, to steal, or at least to beg.

No matter which option they choose, they are always thieves. For, seeing that they became beggars not because of adversity and poverty which was sent to them by God (as He often sends on His servants), but by their own guilt because of their own idleness and negligence, the charity which they receive doesn't belong to them. Therefore they rob from the truly poor—to whom this charity should be given by the commandment of God (Isa. 58:7).

TIMOTHY: Yet there are many who, having arrived at such a place, defend their actions when someone rebukes them for begging, saying: "It's better to beg than to steal."

DANIEL: It is much better for them to do this rather than something worse, but yet they cannot wholly clear themselves from this crime of theft because of the reasons I just mentioned. Therefore it would be good to require them to do more, and it would be best if justice laid hands on such crooks and examined them to know how they lived and why they do not wish to labor. And, if they could give no lawful excuse, they ought to be arrested as thieves.

They ought at least to consider sometime what David said: "I have been young, and now am old; yet have I not seen the righteous forsaken, nor his seed begging bread" (Ps. 37:25). For, though there are often many good people who become poor by the good will of God (who chooses to afflict them with poverty), yet the vast majority of men fall into such a deplorable state by their own fault—that is, because they refuse to submit themselves to the commandment of God by laboring as He has commanded them (Gen. 3:17-19).

TIMOTHY: There are some who defend and excuse themselves in this, saying that they would willingly labor if they could find employment, but they cannot find anyone who will put them to work.

DANIEL: Let them examine themselves to be certain that they have not caused this problem by their dishonesty or laziness. For Solomon had good reason to write: "As vinegar to the teeth, and as smoke to the eyes, so is the sluggard to them that send him" (Prov. 10:26). Thus it should come as no surprise if no one wants to hire such a man.

THE ABUSE WHICH EXISTS IN USING THE NAMES OF VIRTUES FOR VICES BECAUSE SOME ARE MISTAKEN FOR THE OTHERS, AND ABOVE ALL IN THE CIVIL GOVERNMENT; AND THE PUNISHMENT OF GOD UPON THE NEGLIGENT, LAZY, AND WASTEFUL

TIMOTHY: You have discovered their problem. But there is still another point which many people abuse: they give the name of virtue to many vices because of the similarity that these often appear to have with the virtues because of a lack of proper discernment. Thus it happens that the wasteful man is mistaken for a generous soul and the miser for a responsible manager of his goods.

So on the other hand vices are extolled as virtues. Thus it also happens that the responsible manager will be considered a miser and a stingy man by the spendthrift, and the generous man will be looked upon as a wasteful man by the miser and greedy man. It is the same with the diligent and the negligent man, and with the lazy and the hard-working man. For the lazy and negligent will accuse the diligent and good managers (who are not lazy and negligent like themselves) of being stingy men, and will make a mockery of them.

DANIEL: What you say is true. In this we can clearly see the deep corruption within the judgment of men, and above all within civil offices, which are often entrusted either to miserly and avaricious men or to spendthrifts and squanderers who either by negligence or laziness squander the public goods. Some they leave to perish by their negligence, while others they take to enrich themselves, and still others they employ to pay the infinite cost of their prodigality and evil management.

This plague is all too common in our day. But the false image and appearance of virtue with which these vices are painted disguises all, and causes them to be taken for something that they are not, and for the virtues wholly contrary to what they are. By this God executes a great judgment on men when He gives them such thieves, spendthrifts, and robbers as governors.

And with regard to the others who sin by their extravagance, negligence, and laziness, seeing that they are not punished by human laws as they ought to be, God will truly execute the Law that He gave against them by Paul, commanding: "if any would not work, neither should he eat" (1 Thess. 3:10), and will punish them Himself either by scarcity, famines, poverty, and misery, or by the tyranny and plundering of the tyrants who daily charge and impose new taxes on them, whether by loans at exorbitant interest by lenders, or other similar men, which are given them as scourges and executioners. For how many times are they constrained to give their goods at some vile price to such people in order to have such assistance from them in their own time of need?

TIMOTHY: Our daily experience truly testifies that this is the case, for I can assure you that there are some who often endure great hunger and abject poverty who, because they lack money and food (which is an incurable and desperate malady in such people), are forced to suffer hunger and live in self-denial in spite of themselves, though they have no religious purpose for it.

THE VANITY OF THOSE WHO ASCRIBE AND ATTRIBUTE TO THE EFFECTS OF THE CONSTELLATIONS THE WICKEDNESS AND INCLINATIONS TO WHICH MEN ARE SUBJECT AND DISPOSED

DANIEL: If we diligently consider all that we have already dealt with concerning the matter we are discussing at present, it will be easy for us to recognize the vanity of astrologers and those who believe in their astrology, who submit men's spirits, hearts, wills, desires, and inclinations to the effects of the constellations, planets, and stars as if they were the cause of the vices to which men are inclined and subject. Because of this, if it happens that a man or a child is given to theft, fornication, or some other similar wickedness, it is commonly said: "He was born under such-and-such a planet."

TIMOTHY: Many espouse this error.

DANIEL: Doesn't it seem reasonable that we should search in heaven for our own sins and guilt so that we can excuse ourselves and put the blame on such good creations of God and on God who is their Creator? But, according to Moses' testimony, He did not create the stars and planets to induce us by them to commit the evil acts which He forbids us to commit and which are displeasing to Him, but rather He created them "for signs, and for seasons, and for days, and years" (Gen. 1:14).

TIMOTHY: It is true that the stars which induce us to steal are earthly—not heavenly—ones, just as you have shown. That is, they are our own corrupt nature, our unbelief, negligence, laziness, and the other vices we've discussed. We can say the same of all other sins and all transgressions contrary to the Law of God.

CHAPTER SIX

Various Types of Theft

THE CONSIDERATION NECESSARY IN THE DIVISION OF VARIOUS TYPES OF THEFT, AND THE VARIOUS NAMES GIVEN TO THEM, AND THE REASONS WHY

DANIEL: Seeing that all these matters are so amply summarized, let us proceed now to the other point which I promised to deal with after the first. By what we have said you can already understand the true definition and meaning of theft, not only according to lawyers and legislators, but also according to the Word of God. Now we must speak of the division and the various types of theft, which we can consider in various ways.

TIMOTHY: Explain them to me.

DANIEL: We can firstly consider theft according to the persons against whom it is committed; and then according to the substance of the things stolen, or according to the quality and quantity of them; and according to the means and practices by which the theft is committed.

TIMOTHY: Tell me all these things point by point, and give me examples of them all.

DANIEL: We will begin with the qualities of thefts taken from the consideration of the persons against whom they were committed.

If the theft is made of the personal property of a private individual, it is considered simple theft. If it is made against common and public property—that is, of a ruler and a domain or community or commonwealth—the Latins call it *peculat.* If it is something dedicated to God and His church, either for the preservation of its ministry or for the sustenance of His ministers or for the poor over whom it has charge, it is called *sacrilege.*

TIMOTHY: I do not doubt that this diversity of names was employed to distinguish between various degrees of thefts.

DANIEL: This is true. For, though all theft is a great crime before God because His Law and majesty are violated by it, yet the position of the persons greatly adds to or diminishes the crime. Consequently the crime is worthy of much more grievous punishment when it is made against public property rather than against that of a private individual, inasmuch as the one is also much more grievous and more dangerous than the other.

THE TYPE OF THEFT OF PUBLIC GOODS CALLED 'PECULAT,' AND HOW GRIEVOUS IT IS; AND THE REASONS WHY, AND IN WHAT PERSONS IT IS MOST DETESTABLE

TIMOTHY: Yet it seems that we ought to judge completely contrary to what you say, at least in this type of theft which is made against the ruler and a community or commonwealth. For a ruler, a domain, and many joined together could more easily bear and be in less danger at such a loss than a private individual, and particularly a poor man to whom the theft of a single coin would be more damaging than that of a hundred coins to a rich man or a lord and his domain.

DANIEL: What you say has some appearance of truth, and I do not deny that a theft against a poor man is more detestable before God than that committed against a rich man, inasmuch as cruelty is joined to the theft committed against a poor man; therefore it is like a type of murder and highway robbery. But we must not only consider the quality of the grievance and damage, but also the consequences and the impudence and audacity of the thief. For, if he dares to raise himself up against his ruler and against the entire commonwealth and community, how would he carry himself toward private individuals? Doesn't he openly declare that he bears no reverence for anyone, not even for the ruler or his domain, of which he takes so little account?

Secondly, we must consider the preservation of the public order. For if it is violated in an individual person and in a single member only, the united body of the community can aid and remedy it, but when it is committed against the entire body in general, it is also committed against every individual who is a member of this body and who are all violated together; thus the outcome is much wickeder. And if such a theft is committed by the officers themselves who have charge of the public goods and to whom they have been entrusted, it is much more grievous and execrable.

TIMOTHY: This is the same as making the wolf the shepherd, as the common proverb puts it.

DANIEL: Yet there are many such shepherds among the offices and governments and administrations of the public moneys, who ought to be considered similar to the guardians who steal, pillage, and destroy the poor pupils and orphans whom they are given to tutor, if they appropriate to themselves what they ought to preserve for those whom they serve, or to whom they are governors and guardians.

SACRILEGE, AND WHAT IT BEARS WITH IT, AND THE MOST ABOMINABLE SACRILEGE

TIMOTHY: In my opinion, we can also say the same of sacrilege.

DANIEL: It is true. For, firstly, the majesty of God is greatly despised and violated by it, seeing that if the thief who commits sacrilege had any reverence for the God whose goods he steals, he would have more horror of laying his hand on them than on any other (though it would never be lawful for him to steal the goods of another).

Also, just as he who steals the public goods destroys

the community and its public order (as much as he is able), so also sacrilege destroys, as much as it can, the Church and the order which the Lord has established within it. For it cannot be preserved without the ministry by which God wills to preserve it, and without caring for the poor destitute members of Jesus Christ who are within it. Therefore whoever removes the means by which these things must be accomplished and preserved, places the church (as much as he is able), in the danger that we mentioned. For if others acted as he did, what would become of the Church?

Furthermore, if a man is a thief who does not assist the Church or its members by his goods when necessity requires it, how much more must a man be considered as such who, instead of giving, steals the very things that are given by others? And if rulers, who are required to punish sacrilege and be the nursing fathers and nursing mothers of the church (according to Isaiah 49:23), commit sacrilege themselves and steal the church's goods for their own use, or if those who call themselves its pastors and ministers do this, how much more abominable ought we to consider their sacrilege? Yet there are today few of those who call themselves bishops and pastors, and those who have the management of her goods, who have hands truly cleansed from such sacrilege.

CHAPTER SEVEN

The Stealing of Persons

THE CONSIDERATION OF THEFTS IN THE SUBSTANCE OF THE THINGS STOLEN; AND FIRSTLY THOSE WHICH ARE COMMITTED AGAINST THE PERSONS OF MEN, AND THE SELLING OF THEM

TIMOTHY: I now understand these points. Let us proceed to the others; and let us speak firstly of the variety of thefts according to the substance and matter of the things stolen.

DANIEL: The greatest theft, and the most unbearable which can be made in this regard, is when people themselves are stolen. For whoever commits such theft sins against the common nature of men and declares himself an enemy of it. And, if we must judge a theft according to the value of the things stolen, there can be no greater theft, for there is nothing under heaven worth as much as a human being. This is why God issued the death sentence against such thieves, saying: "And he that stealeth a man, and selleth him, or if he be found in his hand, he shall surely be put to death" (Ex. 21:16). The Latins also gave a very fitting name to this type of theft, calling it *plagium*.

After men follows beasts, and then inanimate objects. The theft of a beast also bore its own name among the Latins, and was called *abigeatus*.

TIMOTHY: Explain these things a little more clearly for me, and tell me firstly how you understand the theft of persons.

DANIEL: This can truly be done in various ways. The first is when someone steals a person just as Joseph was taken by his brothers and sold to the Ishmaelites (Gen. 37:23-28). This type of theft is now more common where the slavery of former days is still in existence and where men are made merchandise of just like beasts, as it is among the Turks and the Moors and those who have dealings with them and who follow their methods, as do certain Spaniards and Italians.

THE THEFTS OF YOUNG CHILDREN, AND OF WIVES AND DAUGHTERS AMONG CHRISTIANS

TIMOTHY: Thanks be to God that Christians are delivered from this danger on this point, if they do not dwell among those you mentioned who follow in such a case the manners of the Turks or the ancient pagans.

DANIEL: It is true. Yet this does not prevent many similar thefts from existing among themselves, particularly concerning young children and wives and daughters. (Because of the detestation which I have for them, I will not speak of those who daily live in the wickednesses and abominations of the Sodomites, seeing that this is often the reason why they steal children.) But let us speak of beggars who occasionally steal the very young; then they break their limbs or deform them and carry them through the country, to beg for them and thus provide for themselves in their idleness under the cover and guise of caring for them, as the judgments which have been made by justice in various places bear witness to.

Also, those who steal other peoples' daughters to take them in marriage against the will of their fathers and mothers and relatives and friends, can't they in some way truly be included under this type of theft? And if these deserve to be placed in this rank, what should we say of those who steal them for their own filthy purposes or to place them in prostitution for others? Or those who even abduct and steal married women themselves? What also should we say of those madams and pimps who make merchandise of the young girls stolen and seduced in this way, to sell them as prostitutes?

KIDNAPPINGS COMMITTED BY BRIBERY AND ENTICEMENT AND BY THOSE WHO FOR THEIR OWN PERSONAL GAIN SURRENDER THOSE WHOM GOD HAS PLACED UNDER THEIR CHARGE

TIMOTHY: Besides the theft which is committed by such people in such a case, this wickedness is even more, which we just discussed on the commandment concerning adultery. But it seems to me that there can still be a difference in this case according to the manner in which the thing is done, as we already touched on in the abduction of wives and daughters. For if it is done by force, it seems to me that the crime is much more grievous than if the person abducted and stolen went with consent and of their own free will.

DANIEL: It is true. But there is always theft involved in every person who in any way abducts and entices people who are under the guard and protection of another without the knowledge and will of those whom God has placed over them; such that we can here place such a difference between them as between outright theft and fraud, which are both thefts, though they are different types of it.

TIMOTHY: And if those who have charge of them sell them, or if they sell themselves for the reason that we have given, aren't they also kidnappers?

DANIEL: Yes, because they sell what they do not own. For, though God has placed them in their power, yet He did not give them permission to abuse them and treat them in this way, but He placed them in their charge for the opposite reason, and to protect them from such dangers. Therefore neither the father himself—nor the mother—exercises such power over their own children.

TIMOTHY: Rightly so, for by doing this they would show themselves to be not fathers and mothers, but worse than thieves and brothel-keepers.

KIDNAPPINGS WORTHY OF PRAISE

DANIEL: There are some kidnappings which are not only permissible, but are also praiseworthy, as that which Jehosheba daughter of King Joram committed when she kidnapped her nephew the son of Ahaziah her brother, of which it is written: "And when Athaliah the mother of Ahaziah saw that her son was dead, she arose and destroyed all the seed royal. But Jehosheba . . . took Joash the son of Ahaziah, and stole him from among the king's sons which were slain; and they hid him, even him and his nurse, in the bedchamber from Athaliah, so that he was not slain" (2 Kings 11:1-2). We can also add to this example that of the midwives who concealed the children of the Hebrews in Egypt and did not reveal them, but "saved the men children alive" so that Pharaoh would not kill them (Ex. 1:17). Obadiah did the same, who "took an hundred prophets, and hid them by fifty in a cave, and fed them with bread and water" so that Jezebel could not find and kill them (1 Kings 18:4).

TIMOTHY: The example of Tobit, who secretly buried the bodies of his brethren at the peril of his own life, is somewhat similar to these.

DANIEL: Would that it pleased God today that there were many such thieves who, by righteous means, might steal believers from the tyrants who pursue them to death, instead of the brigands who now lend a hand in their slaughter!

THEFTS OF BEASTS

TIMOTHY: We have now sufficiently discussed kidnappings and thefts of persons. What do you say to the theft of beasts?

DANIEL: This includes not only those who steal beasts which they take to kill or sell, but those also who steal them to make use of them themselves, or who harm them and prevent them—in whatever way they might—from rendering to their masters the labor and benefit they should receive from them. For this reason the Lord expressly mentions the ox and donkey in His Law (which were the primary animals by which men were then served in their plowing and in obtaining their food), and commands that if anyone finds one going astray, he must take it and return it to its masters, and that if it has fallen under its burden he must help it to right itself—indeed, even when it belongs to his very enemy (Ex. 23:4-5; Deut. 22:4).

By this He shows us that, not only is he a thief who takes the goods of another, but also whoever does not assist his neighbor according to the power which God has given him. This person has not fulfilled this commandment of which I now speak, even though he might not have rendered any harm to his neighbor's animal.

CHAPTER EIGHT

Thefts of Food, Money, and the Word of God

THEFTS OF INANIMATE OBJECTS, AND THOSE COMMITTED EITHER IN THE SUBSTANCE OR IN THE QUALITY OF THINGS

TIMOTHY: Let us now proceed to the other point, which is inanimate objects, and let us speak firstly of their substance and material.

DANIEL: A theft is committed in substance and in material when one is exchanged for the other, as if a man gave silver for gold, or copper for silver, or lead for copper, exchanging one material for the other. We can also add to these those people who debase metals and corrupt materials, as when a man mixes water with wine or counterfeits money. For, in doing this, he sells water as wine and gives debased money as true currency.

TIMOTHY: There are many who are thieves in this way. But what also do you say concerning the quality of things?

DANIEL: This is when the theft is committed in such a way that the substance and the material of the thing in which it is committed remains what it is, but there is some fault or defect in it which the seller conceals in such a way that what is faulty and blemished is accepted as good and legitimate. This is a theft because the buyer receives the damage, inasmuch as the merchandise is not of such a quality as it ought to be, like when a man sells rotten, diseased, or worm-eaten wheat (or the refuse of the wheat, as is spoken in Amos 8:6), or sour or stale wine for good. For, though the substance and material are not changed (as if someone sold rye or barley for wheat or lead for copper), yet even so it is not such as it ought to be, nor is it what the buyer believes he is receiving. This is the same as if you sold a worthless beast for a good one.

THEFTS COMMITTED IN QUANTITY AND IN WEIGHTS AND MEASURES OF THINGS BOUGHT OR SOLD, AND HOW THIS MATTER OF THEFT IS CONSIDERED DETESTABLE IN THE HOLY SCRIPTURES

TIMOTHY: I understand this well. Let us speak now of quantity.

DANIEL: The theft is made in it when the measures and weights are false. For, though the substance and the matter is such as it ought to be and of such a quality as is required, yet the amount is diminished. Therefore there is not as much as there should be. Thus it follows that whatever is lacking is stolen from him who purchases the goods. This type of theft is strongly condemned—very many times—in the Holy Scriptures.

TIMOTHY: This theft is also very frequent and quite common because it is much easier to steal from men by this means than to alter the substance and materials or to corrupt them, because it is much easier to perceive the deception in such an alteration or corruption than it is in this matter of weights and measures. For, when we buy or sell, we must for the most part trust the weights and measures of the merchants with whom we deal. For we cannot always carry our own weights and measures with us.

DANIEL: Because of this, the iniquity of those who falsify it is so much greater because they so wickedly deceive those who trust in them. By this they are like public thieves and highway robbers. This is why it is written: "Thou shalt not have in thy bag divers weights, a great and a small. Thou shalt not have in thine house divers measures, a great and a small. But thou shalt have a perfect and just weight, a perfect and just measure shalt thou have: that thy days may be lengthened in the land which the LORD thy God giveth thee. For all that do such things, and all that do unrighteously, are an abomination unto the LORD thy God" (Deut. 25:13-16).

And in Leviticus: "Ye shall do no unrighteousness in judgment, in meteyard, in weight, or in measure. Just balances, just weights, a just ephah, and a just hin, shall ye have" (Lev. 19:35-36).

And in Proverbs: "Divers weights, and divers measures, both of them are alike abomination to the LORD," but "a just weight is His delight" (Prov. 20:10; 11:1).

And if this deception is so greatly displeasing to God, it is even worse when someone both diminishes the weights and measures and also raises the price, against which the Lord brought an accusation by His prophet Amos, saying: "Hear this, O ye that swallow up the needy, even to make the poor of the land to fail, saying, When will the new moon be gone, that we may sell corn? and the sabbath, that we may set forth wheat, making the ephah small, and the shekel great, and falsifying the balances by deceit? That we may buy the poor for silver, and the needy for a pair of shoes; yea, and sell the refuse of the wheat?" (Amos 8:4-6.)

This is how the Lord records the accusation against such inveterate thieves. And then He pronounces—indeed, with an oath—the sentence of punishment and vengeance which He will bring upon them, saying: "The LORD hath sworn by the excellency of Jacob, Surely I will never forget any of their works. Shall not the land tremble for this, and every one mourn that dwelleth therein?" (Amos 8:7-8.) I will refrain from quoting the rest of what the prophet says on this point.

THE INVENTION AND USE OF MONEY, AND COUNTERFEITERS; AND THE MAGNITUDE OF THIS CRIME, AND THE THEFT COMMITTED BY SUCH MEANS

TIMOTHY: What sort of people do you think are the guiltiest in these things, and who cause the most harm by them?

DANIEL: The number of them is so great that I find it exceedingly difficult to respond to your question. Nevertheless I can give you a few types and examples.

Firstly, counterfeiters are very dangerous and harmful. This is because money and the type of money (gold, silver, and other metals) has been employed by men to more easily conduct business and to have the easiest means of sharing with one another the goods which God has given them. For the course of commercial dealings is nothing more than an exchange made between men by which some give to others something they possess, and accept something else in payment, according to the value of the goods exchanged. Now, because it is very difficult to transport the things which we have for trade, money is used instead of them, according to the price they are valued at, which is truly much easier to carry and much more fitting than anything else for all kinds of trade and merchandise.

Therefore, seeing that God has given this means to man so that they can assist each other more easily, those who pervert and confound this order are a grave scourge to the public good and to all human society. Thus they are worthy of grievous punishment, and this even more so because they create such terrible confusion among men. For men cannot live without trading with each other. Therefore whoever removes this means is like a public criminal who slits the throat of the entire community of mankind, for by his fraud he destroys the trust and honesty without which human society can neither exist nor be preserved. For, if trust and honesty are removed, no one can be sure of anything. Therefore by this men live in terrible trouble and in a disorder the like of which has never been surpassed.

Now there are perhaps none who create a more terrible disorder in this way than counterfeiters. For, besides the fact that they are public thieves who rob from the entire community of mankind, they also confound the public order by rebelling against the authority and rights of the rulers to whom the power of coining money and fixing its value is given to maintain this order and public peace, which could not be maintained in such justice and equity as is required if it were lawful for every man to coin money after his own whims.

TIMOTHY: Thus, on this point, not only are the counterfeiters guilty who coin false currency and who debase it, but also those who coin lawful currency without proper authority, inasmuch as by this they attribute to themselves that which rightly pertains to their rulers.

DANIEL: It is true. But there is a difference in this, for he who not only confounds the public order but also robs the entire community sins much more grievously than the other.

THIEVES AND COUNTERFEITERS OF THE WORD OF GOD, AND THE THEFTS WHICH THEY MAKE BOTH OF MEN AND THEIR POSSESSIONS BY THIS MEANS

TIMOTHY: If these are so dangerous and are punished so grievously, what can we say of those who counterfeit the Word of God, which is the true spiritual stamp and currency of His people for the preservation of the Church and spiritual life?

DANIEL: It is easy to judge this. Jeremiah calls the false prophets "thieves of the Word of God" because they stole the Word from the people of God by falsifying it like forgers and by setting forth their dreams and inventions instead of it. Therefore he said in the name of the Lord: "Therefore, behold, I am against the prophets, saith the LORD, that steal My words every one from his neighbour. Behold, I am against the prophets, saith the LORD, that use their tongues, and say, He saith. Behold, I am against them that prophesy false dreams, saith the LORD, and do tell them, and cause My people to err by their lies, and by their lightness; yet I sent them not, nor commanded them: therefore they shall not profit this people at all, saith the LORD" (Jer. 23:30-32).

Not only can we truly call these men thieves of all sorts, but also murderers of souls.

Firstly, they are kidnappers because they entice and steal men's hearts by their false doctrine, and steal them from God by this means. They also murder their souls because they cause them to be deprived of eternal life.

Secondly, they steal their eternal inheritance as well as their earthly goods, which are the main reasons why they do this.

TIMOTHY: Yet there are many such thieves and falsifiers upon the earth.

DANIEL: At least the entire kingdom of the Roman antichrist is well supplied with them, inasmuch as it has no other prophets than such thieves and counterfeiters who have wholly overturned and falsified the teaching of the Lord and perverted the sacraments ordained by Him.

TIMOTHY: I agree with you. But how I wish that such men were not also found among those who boast themselves of the purity of the Gospel! For it is not enough to preach without mixing in false doctrine, but it is also required to preach the Word in its entirety, without concealing anything out of fear of men or in an effort to please them.

DANIEL: How good it would be if this were not so! But we will go no further on this path at present, but instead pursue what we have begun.

THOSE WHO CLIP COINS AND USE MONEY WHICH THEY KNOW IS NOT GENUINE; AND PARTICULARLY THOSE WHO HAVE CHARGE OF PUBLIC MONEYS

TIMOTHY: It seems to me that we could rightly add to the counterfeiters all those who clip coins and who diminish their weight, and who use false and unjust weights knowingly, and not by ignorance, as often happens. For, though these work differently than those called counterfeiters, yet, seeing that their deeds tend nearly to the same end as the others, they all end up at the same place even though the means are somewhat different.

DANIEL: You touch upon a matter in which the hands of those who have the management of public moneys are often as stained as the others. When they receive money, they are meticulous in checking to be sure that each coin has its full weight and value and that nothing is debased, and that nothing is missing and the money has not been miscounted. But, when it comes time to disburse and pay the salaries of those who have served either in the church or for the public good, or to give something to the poor, God knows with what loyalty and faithfulness they do their job.

TIMOTHY: I have known some who would (as I think) make a great conscience of never making a full payment to those whom they dealt with, and particularly to the poor, without always retaining some portion either of the wages that were due them or of the charity which was commanded them, and they do this either by using counterfeit money or unjust weights, or spurious bills. They also think that the poor ought not to complain, even though they are so openly robbed and cheated.

DANIEL: These are not only thieves and counterfeiters, but are also swindlers and public menaces, worse than those who rob a man in the woods. For what worse could they do besides taking away their very life?

TIMOTHY: Yet they never receive what is owed them from those who make them payments without counting it properly or weighing and testing it, not in the sort that they give to others who do not have the boldness to resist their tyranny and theft.

DANIEL: You can be assured of this.

CORRUPTIONS BY BRIBES OR GIFTS, AND MERCHANTS WHO BUY AND SELL JUSTICE AND THE POOR

TIMOTHY: Therefore I would be astonished that they made so much gold and silver unlawfully if I did not consider a means by which so much came into their hands. It is certain that they do just as we said when they ask and receive these as a debt. But, seeing that they are men who are able to sell both God and

His people and Church, and faith, justice, and righteousness, in consideration of this, buyers will never fail to appear, and we cannot doubt that they will receive much gold and silver beyond measure, which is given them as a gift to pervert justice and to sell the poor and the Church of God. For such merchants always find enough buyers to pay them; but what is even worse, the buyers make them sellers. For, if the buyers did not seek out such sellers, I think that the sellers would exhibit more shame in soliciting such buyers. Therefore the buyers are no less guilty than the sellers (if they are not more so).

DANIEL: You have hit the mark. For I truly think that these merchants are not so shameless as to make a difficulty of receiving debased gold and silver which is given them as a gift, without weighing it.

TIMOTHY: You can truly see that they practice the common proverb: "Don't look a gift horse in the mouth."

DANIEL: Doubtless so. And concerning what you said about the buyers, it does seem to me that we ought to judge them greater and more dangerous thieves than the sellers. It seems to me that we can place the same difference between a madam and a brothel-keeper and a woman solicited by them. For, though the woman who allows herself to be seduced by their solicitations is worthy of great condemnation and infamy, yet he who solicits her is the main cause of the evil which she does, and the instigator of it.

THEFTS COMMITTED IN THE SALE OF FOODS, AND THE DANGERS IN ITS CORRUPTIONS

TIMOTHY: What you say is true. Tell me now of others who seem to be the most dangerous and who cause the greatest harm to men in the theft of the quality and quantity of things.

DANIEL: They would be those who make merchandise of food and provisions. But those who cheat in the quality are much more dangerous than those who cheat in the quantity. For it often happens that, in order to earn a penny or two, they kill not only a single man, but an entire family.

TIMOTHY: What do you mean by this?

DANIEL: If you go to the market or the butcher and instead of a good fish someone sells you a rotten or a spoiled one, or instead of fresh meat they sell you something decaying or sell you some beast that is dying of some dangerous disease, or even if they only sell you sheep for mutton or beef, or a kid too young, you are in danger of catching some disease or getting sick with some deadly illness which will take away your life, or which will at least cause you grave trouble and place you in grave danger, and will cost you a great deal both of your body and goods.

TIMOTHY: I have often seen many such risks as you describe happen by such means.

DANIEL: Though it may seem that this would be no great theft, yet it can certainly happen that a man prone to some disease, or who otherwise is small and of a weak constitution, if he is exposed to such dangers, will die. And, with him dead, it is almost the same as if his wife and children had all had their throats slit, for they have lost their provider and will fall into need and dangers and hardships much worse than death, seeing that he who ought to provide them food has been snatched away from them. Thus the thief who, in order to gain a little money, is the cause of all this mischief, is not only a thief, but also a shameless criminal and a murderer, worse than those who rob and murder secretly, for he robs men in public places and in plain sight.

Therefore theft and all robbery are often rightly called by the name of "blood" and "murder" in the Holy Scriptures because of the similarity that these crimes have to one another and because of the consequences they bear with them (Isa. 1:15-17, 21-23). Now if such harm can happen by only having sold one type of meat for another, what danger is there if the foods which are daily sold are wholly corrupted and dangerous by nature?

TIMOTHY: This is truly the same as he who sells poison instead of good medicine. Therefore it seems to me that such thieves must be considered not only as thieves, but also as poisoners and public menaces.

THE CARE WHICH MAGISTRATES MUST HAVE OVER FOOD, AND THE GREAT DESPISING OF OATHS EXISTING BECAUSE OF THEM

DANIEL: This is why rulers and magistrates and all their officers must keep a watchful eye on such things, for they are unbelievably dangerous and damaging. And if they punish poisoners who poison individual people, ought they not also to punish those who poison the public at large, and who do it publicly?

TIMOTHY: There are also many occupations in which an oath is given to sell good and wholesome foods and to use honest weights and measures, as are the butchers in many countries, and others likewise in various localities.

DANIEL: It is true. But there are few who pay any great heed to such an oath. There are many who execute their office no more faithfully than if they had taken no oath at all, or than if they had sworn to do the very opposite of what their duty and office required. For, as Jesus Christ says: "He that is faithful in that which is least is faithful also in much: and he that is unjust in the least is unjust also in much" (Luke 16:10). Thus it readily follows that he whose conscience does not trouble him in one thing will have no great trouble in any other.

TIMOTHY: Thus if perjury is joined to theft, the theft is much more detestable.

DANIEL: It is easy to see that two sins are more grievous than one alone, and particularly when the majesty of God is so exceedingly desecrated as it is in perjury.

THE GUILT OF MAGISTRATES AND OFFICERS IN THIS REGARD, BY WHICH THEY MAKE THEMSELVES GUILTY OF THE THEFTS AND WICKEDNESSES WHICH ARE COMMITTED IN THESE THINGS

TIMOTHY: If rulers, magistrates, and officers watched over such affairs as their duty requires, there would not be such a great disorder as there is. But they display a great negligence and carelessness toward these things.

DANIEL: It is true. But the evil is still much greater in the corruption which is in them, of which we have already spoken. For, because the vast majority of them can be bought by gold and silver and by gifts and presents, all the wicked—and above all, the greatest thieves—take much greater boldness to do everything they please. For, as the common proverb says, "He who has his ruler as an accomplice can afford to be an excellent thief."

Therefore why would a master of money and a forger be concerned if they made a thousand counterfeits by which they gained infinite riches? For they know that either they will be discovered or they will not be. If they are not discovered (as often happens), all is theirs. And if they are discovered, they have the money in hand to bribe the magistrates and his officers. If they have stolen thirty thousand dollars, they could corrupt many judges, magistrates, and officers if they desired to employ ten or twelve thousand to do it. For how many officials will they find who desire and expect nothing else, and who make the majority of their money by such practices? When this is done, *voila!* the master counterfeiter and the forger and thief escape, and keep all the remains of their theft, provided that they have shared some portion of the spoils with their accomplices.

TIMOTHY: I also find a grievous sin in the rulers in the custom they have now taken in many places of selling the offices of justice, and that very dearly. For, besides the covetousness and greediness natural to men, there is besides this the problem that the merchant who purchases it must sell to repay himself for the money he has stolen.

DANIEL: You pass by another evil, which is that, when the offices are sold or given by corruption, the worthiest men do not get them, but those who give the most, who are often the most wicked. By this rulers render themselves guilty of all the evils which happen because they did not remedy these things as they ought to have done.

THE DANGER OF DOCTORS AND PHYSICIANS IN SUCH MATTERS, AND THE LAW WHICH GOD GAVE CONCERNING WEIGHTS AND MEASURES, AND HIS THREATENINGS AGAINST THOSE WHO FALSIFY THEM

TIMOTHY: It seems to me that it is also very necessary for doctors and those who make medicines to diligently heed their consciences in such a case. For, just as they can give great assistance to men when they do as they ought to, so also there are no murderers or poisoners more dangerous than them, if they are such; seeing that they hold a person's life and death in their hands. And it is often no great matter for them to take away or preserve life, particularly in the matter of medicines. You said that there was greater danger from thefts committed in the quality of things than in those which are made in the quantity, but it seems to me that great iniquities are also committed in weights and measures, and that the thefts which are here committed are extremely dangerous and damaging.

DANIEL: You can easily judge by what we already saw from the Holy Scriptures. The Lord did not say without reason: "Thou shalt not have in thy bag divers weights, [or] in thine house" (Deut. 25:13-14). For there are many who sell and deliver by one weight and measure, and who purchase and receive by another.

And because there are various sorts of merchandise and measures, the Lord specified them according to their diversities. Therefore He makes mention of *weights, measures, ephahs,* and *hins,* by which He includes all other sorts of weights and measures both of liquids and solids (Lev. 19:36). For vast falsifications are committed in all types. Therefore the Lord said that whoever does such things is "an abomination" (Deut. 25:16). Thus it follows that He holds such people in great detestation, which is a position to be feared worse than death. For what more could we fear than God's indignation against us, who holds our very life and death in His hand? He also says that He is against all injustice. Thus it rightly follows that He is the enemy of all those who commit injustice, and that He will work His vengeance upon them Himself (Heb. 10:30-31; Rom. 12:19).

TIMOTHY: I do not doubt it.

DANIEL: Indeed, we cannot doubt it, for God has given the sentence from His own mouth. And therefore we must not judge thefts according to man's judgment only, but according to the judgment and justice of God. For, no matter what men may judge, God will not abide by their judgment, but by His, and He will not change His justice to follow theirs. For there is an infinity of thefts which never come to man's knowledge. Therefore the thieves who commit them remain unpunished among us.

Also, there are as many types of theft (including some that we have already mentioned) which, far from being considered thefts, and far from the thieves who are guilty of them being taken for thieves and being punished, instead they are considered the most noble, notable, and honorable among men, and receive the highest places—not by the scaffold, by which they ought to receive the highest place—but are considered worthy of the highest honors and dignity. This is how men work, but all is not so. For they must still pass through God's hands, who is their sovereign Judge, and He cannot lie or deny Himself or violate His Law in His judgments.

CHAPTER NINE

Robbers and Robbery

OTHER TYPES OF THEFTS CONSIDERED ACCORDING TO THE FORM AND MANNER IN WHICH THEY ARE COMMITTED, AND FIRSTLY OF ROBBERY

TIMOTHY: Seeing that we have spoken of various types of thefts according to the substance and matter stolen, and then according to the quantity and quality of the things stolen and according to the consideration of persons from whom they are stolen, I now wish for us to speak of the other types still left to be considered according to the method, form, and manner of stealing.

DANIEL: When something is stolen and hidden without the knowledge and will of its owner, you know what name we must put to the crime. However, if it is stolen by open violence, within the sight and knowledge of its owner, this is *robbery,* and he who commits it is a *robber.* A robber is much worse than a simple thief, for robbery is not only a type of theft, but is also a crime shamelessly committed in public. In this act there is a much greater contempt of justice and all human society, and a much greater evil than in other types of theft. For, seeing that the thief fears to be discovered in his theft, he comes in secret, and if he cannot steal secretly, he flees. Therefore if we are watchful over our affairs, and if we take the necessary precautions, thieves will not harm us. But being watchful counts for nothing against a robber, nor can all the precautions that you might take, if you are not stronger than he is, for he will take everything you possess from before your very eyes, and care not at all that you see him.

THOSE WHO ARE MOST GIVEN TO ROBBERY; AND IN WHAT CONSIDERATION ROBBERS OUGHT TO BE HELD AMONG MEN; AND THEIR PUNISHMENT

TIMOTHY: Who do you suppose are those who are must subject to such a crime?

DANIEL: All tyrants and those who are strong and powerful, who rob, confiscate, and carry away the possessions of others by force. In doing this they are no different than highwaymen who kill and pillage men in the lanes and woods, for they have no more right to do what they do except that they are stronger, and because they hinder the course of justice by their power and their prey are not rescued from their hands, which is a crime which the poor and those who are less than or equal to us dare not attempt. Therefore, if they desire to have our possessions in spite of our wishes, they must steal them in secret and clandestinely.

TIMOTHY: They are then like savage beasts and birds of prey among the other beasts and birds.

DANIEL: It is true. Job speaks of them when he says: "Some remove the landmarks; they violently take away flocks, and feed thereof. They drive away the ass of the fatherless, they take the widow's ox for a pledge. They turn the needy out of the way: the poor of the earth hide themselves together. Behold, as wild asses in the desert, go they forth to their work; rising betimes for a prey: the wilderness yieldeth food for them and for their children. They reap every one his corn in the field: and they gather the vintage of the wicked. They cause the naked to lodge without clothing, that they have no covering in the cold. They are wet with the showers of the mountains, and embrace the rock for want of a shelter. They pluck the fatherless from the breast, and take a pledge of the poor. They cause him to go naked without clothing, and they take away the sheaf from the hungry; which make oil within their walls, and tread their winepresses, and suffer thirst. Men groan from out of the city, and the soul of the wounded crieth out" (Job 24:2-12).

Because of this the prophet compares such people to wolves and lions, whom Ezekiel speaks of in this way: "Her princes in the midst thereof are like wolves ravening the prey, to shed blood, and to destroy souls, to get dishonest gain" (Eze. 22:27). And Zephaniah: "Her princes within her are roaring lions" (Zeph. 3:3).

We can place in this category illegal taxations, exactions, and extortions by which people are robbed and burdened without just cause. On this we must note that if God has forbidden simple theft, which is a lesser crime than robbery, with how much greater force has He forbidden this, which is a much greater crime, by forbidding that which is lesser?

And, seeing that He has forbidden it, tyrants and robbers must not think that by their power and violence they will escape the punishment they deserve. For they must answer to God who has forbidden them from doing these acts, who is much stronger than they are and who will easily find other thieves, brigands, and robbers to serve Him as their executioners and to pay them back in their own coin. We see Him do this daily by means of wars, which often accomplish what the Lord said: "Woe to thee that spoilest, . . . [for] thou shalt be spoiled" (Isa. 33:1). And, even though they may escape in this world, yet they will not get off scot-free for all that.

THOSE WHO RETAIN THE DEBTS THEY OWE AND THE WAGES OF THOSE WHO WORK FOR THEM, AND HOW DISPLEASING THIS IS TO GOD

TIMOTHY: Can we not also rightly add to these all those who by force retain the debts they owe and the wages of those who labor for them?

DANIEL: Doubtless so, for how are they any different from those who take a man's wallet by force? For, if I lend you money and you keep it against my will, it is just the same as if you took it out of my wallet before my very eyes. Therefore it is written in the Law: "Ye shall not steal, neither deal falsely, neither lie one to another. . . . Thou shalt not defraud thy neighbour, neither rob him: the wages of him that is hired shall not abide with thee all night until the morning" (Lev. 19:11, 13).

You see here how the Lord joins together *stealing, withholding wages,* and *lying* to one's neighbor. And if you withhold the reward of my labor, you do the same as if you were to remove the blood from my body and the energy which I have given in your service. This is why God so expressly commands that: "the wages of him that is hired shall not abide with thee all night until the morning," in order that he to whom it is due might not lack (Deut. 24:15). This is why we are so expressly forbidden to withhold it. On this James says: "Behold, the hire of the labourers who have reaped down your fields, which is of you kept back by fraud, crieth: and the cries of them which have reaped are entered into the ears of the Lord of sabaoth" (Jam. 5:4).

TIMOTHY: Yet there are many who not only withhold them, but also threaten, insult, strike, and beat the poor people who ask for their wages.

DANIEL: I am acquainted with enough of these men.

TIMOTHY: But above all, these are very bold, who reproach them, saying: "You rogue, have you nothing more to eat than this?" They couldn't care less if, by doing this, they force them to become rogues in truth, or if they force them to fast without the commandment of the holy mother church.

THEFTS COMMITTED BY FRAUD AND DECEPTION

DANIEL: There are also many other types of thefts which are committed by cunning and subtlety. These thefts are called *frauds* and *deceptions.* They are different from those we call simply *thefts* because they are committed more openly. So also they differ from robberies because robberies are always committed by violence, but these are committed by subtle means and by cunning practices by which the craftiest and the most cunning deceive the ignorant and innocent in such a way that they convince them to agree with what they intend, despite the fact that the thing is exceedingly harmful and damaging to those who are deceived by them.

But there are various types of frauds and deceptions, for some are more malicious and more villainous than others, though there is some amount of wickedness and villainy in all of them. There is no difference between them except that some are attractive and concealed in better hues and more pleasing practices than others.

TIMOTHY: Explain this to me a little more clearly by giving some examples.

DANIEL: If some poor simple-minded person, not knowing the price of a particular piece of merchandise, addressed himself to a cunning merchant, and if the merchant, seeing the ignorance and naiveté of the man, took advantage of him because of his greediness and sold his merchandise for two or three times the price that it was worth, we must not doubt that such a merchant is a true thief indeed. There is no difference between him and the others except in the method of theft.

This is the same as a man who buys something at a ridiculously low price either from a child or from some other ignorant person who likewise does not know the price at which it should sell. The same is true of all contracts made by fraud which are harmful and damaging to one of the parties involved.

HOW FRAUD AND DECEPTION ARE A FORM OF ROBBERY, ESPECIALLY TOWARD THOSE WHO ARE CONSTRAINED BY NECESSITY TO CONDUCT BUSINESS AND ENTER INTO CONTRACTS TO THEIR GREAT HARM

TIMOTHY: Those who do this are men of wicked consciences and, in my opinion, there is no great difference between them and the robbers whom we just spoke of except that instead of the robbers who use force and violence, the deceivers use crafty treachery by which they mislead and entice those whom they steal from in such a way that they consent to the theft committed against them, without perceiving or recognizing that they have been robbed.

DANIEL: It is true.

TIMOTHY: And what do you say of those who buy at an absurdly low price from persons whom they see to be constrained by poverty and need, knowing quite well that their necessity constrains them to sell what they have at whatever price the buyer desires because they have no other means of obtaining money? This happens far too often, and particularly in times of hardship and famine, just as we heard previously from Amos the prophet (Amos 8:4-6).

DANIEL: Such buyers are true cutthroats and villains. Therefore they are more deserving to be placed among the robbers and tyrants we previously discussed than among the deceivers. There is only one difference between them and the other robbers: though they use force and violence, yet this force and violence is more covert because they force those with whom they do business (by the necessity they are in) to testify by contracts made with them that they have willingly entered into these contracts and were well-advised in what they did. For, though the poor people are not in agreement with what has been done, and are aware of the great damage which such contracts will bring them, yet they dare not say so, nor do anything to show their disagreement.

CHAPTER TEN

Usury, Loans, and the Law of Love

USURERS AND USURY, AND HOW THEY ARE FORBIDDEN IN THE LAW OF GOD, AND WHAT LENDING IS, PROPERLY SPEAKING

TIMOTHY: I think that we can also truly add to these the vast majority of lenders, and all those who make wicked contracts.

DANIEL: When everything is well considered, it is at least difficult to find any strongly apparent reasons to excuse the theft of unjust lenders. Therefore it was not without good reason that the Lord so often forbade this of His people with such explicit laws. For, if our brethren are in need, we are not only bound to lend to them according to the ability which God has given us, but we must also give to them without hope of even receiving back the principal of the loan. For, if we are commanded to give to those who have need, we have much greater reason to lend to them (Deut. 15:1-4, 7-10; Mat. 5:42).

If they have no need and we are willing to lend to them in order that they might make a greater gain and that we might also receive some profit from their industriousness, then, strictly speaking, we must not call it *lending* in the manner that we have used the word here. For we understand it in such a way that we presuppose a need, seeing that the true fountain and source of lending proceeds from necessity.

If there is no urgent need, or if my neighbor is able by himself and from himself to repay what I give him and to offer me some profit without harming himself, that is another matter altogether. For I am not bound to lend to those who have no need any more than I am bound to give them something. But we can truly make an exchange of goods from what the Lord has given to each of us, to aid in advancing each other, on condition that the rule of true charity moderates all. Therefore some contracts which we make are made without violating the nature of the things created by God and without confounding and perverting the manner of living commanded by Him among men, and without introducing wicked examples into human society and violating the laws of love, which must be the true standard of all contracts.

LENDING WHICH IS PERMITTED BY CIVIL LAWS AND BY CHRISTIAN MAGISTRATES, AND THE JUSTICE AND REASON WHICH IS FOUND IN THEM, AND THE MATTERS TO CONSIDER ON THIS

TIMOTHY: If this is so, then the civil laws given by wise and prudent men, both by certain pagan emperors, kings, rulers and magistrates, and also by Christians—indeed, even by those who accept the reformation of the Gospel—which permit certain types of interest-bearing loans by limiting their rates and percentages, are correct?

DANIEL: You must understand that all which is permitted by these civil laws (indeed, even by the most Christian rulers in the world) are not always conformable to the perfection and love which God requires of us in His Law and which Jesus Christ requires of true Christians. For they often permit many things because of the hardness of men's hearts, just as Moses permitted divorce. He did not approve of it as a good thing in and of itself when he allowed it, as appears by the response which Jesus Christ made to the scribes and Pharisees on this matter (Deut. 24:1; Mat. 19:3-8).

TIMOTHY: Why then did he allow it?

DANIEL: In the first place, he did it to avoid another even worse evil, and likewise to relieve poor wives by delivering them from the cruel tyranny of their husbands and from the dangers to which they could be exposed if they were forced to keep them against their conscience.

Thus, to apply this example to our purpose, if there were such love among Christians as there ought to be and as God requires of them, there would be no need to discuss ungodly interest. For every man would be ready not only to lend to another, but also to give his money away when need required it, as the former Christians did in the early Church (Acts 2:44-45; 4:32-35). But there are two things which greatly hinder this.

The first is the hardness of heart of rich men without love, who could easily lend if they wanted to; but the will is not according to power, seeing that they do not have such compassion upon their brethren as they ought.

The other is the unfaithfulness and dishonesty of those to whom we lend, which God punishes in this way. For the perversity of the human heart is so great that you can scarcely lend to anyone without making them your enemy when it comes time for repayment, and without receiving damage and displeasure from him instead of the pleasure and service that you have rendered him, and without having great quarrels and onerous legal proceedings before you can get back your principal, which you are often unable to recover. This is the reason why even the best and most charitable men themselves are very hesitant to lend, and why the poor who are trustworthy and honest often suffer and endure difficulties because of the unfaithfulness and dishonesty of others.

TIMOTHY: There is nothing truer than what you have just said.

DANIEL: For this reason it was necessary for the magistrates to issue laws to provide some remedy, as best as they could find, against all these evils, both to put some cap to the greed and extortions of the rich and greedy as well as to provide some means of assistance to the poor who are scarcely able to borrow if those from whom they borrow do not receive some profit from them.

TIMOTHY: Indeed, in a manner of speaking, fathers will not even lend to their sons!

THE COMMANDMENT BY WHICH JESUS CHRIST REQUIRES CHRISTIANS TO LEND TO ONE ANOTHER; AND IN WHAT WAY WE ARE REQUIRED TO DO THIS; AND THE MEANS BY WHICH CHRISTIANS CAN LEND MONEY ON INTEREST ACCORDING TO GOD, AND PROFIT FROM IT

DANIEL: We can understand by this that very few are found who are led by such love and who desire to follow the instruction which Jesus Christ gave to Christians concerning this matter, saying: "Lend, hoping for nothing again" (Luke 6:35).

TIMOTHY: How do you understand this passage? Do you mean that He commands us to lend without hope of even recovering the principal itself, or without hope of receiving any profit other than the principal?

DANIEL: It is quite certain that we are bound (as we have already said) not only to lend, but also to give when the need of our neighbor requires it (1 John 3:17). But, seeing that Jesus Christ is not speaking in this passage of giving, but of lending, I think it is more suitable to take the meaning of Jesus Christ's words and the matter He deals with in this passage as referring to the profit which we might expect when we lend to someone (as also the Greek word which Luke uses in this place seems to point to). For Jesus Christ clearly declared to His disciples in this sermon what perfection is required of the Christian, and how he must be different from others in his manner of living and in assisting all those who have need—indeed, even his very enemies. For, as He says, if His disciples only lend and do good to those from whom they have received some reward or service or from whom they hope to receive it, how are their actions any better than other men, indeed, even than pagans and unbelievers themselves? (Mat. 5:42-48; Luke 6:30-35).

TIMOTHY: Thus He desires us to lend, having sole regard to the will of God who commends our brethren to our care, and to the need of our neighbors, without considering our own gain or profit, according to what is written: "If there be among you a poor man of one of thy brethren, . . . thou shalt not harden thine heart, nor shut thine hand from thy poor brother: but thou shalt open thine hand wide unto him, and shalt surely lend him sufficient for his need" (Deut. 15:7-8).

DANIEL: It is doubtless so. This is why in another place He advises us to invite to dinner those who cannot repay the good that we show them, in order that God might repay it (Luke 14:13-14). For, as it is written: "He that hath pity upon the poor lendeth unto the LORD; and that which he hath given will He pay him again" (Prov. 19:17).

For, seeing that the poor cannot repay you, God (whom you truly serve when you are serving the poor) will repay you with great profit and vast gains. Therefore it is written in another place: "There is that scattereth, and yet increaseth; and there is that withholdeth more than is meet, but it tendeth to poverty. The liberal soul shall be made fat: and he that watereth shall be watered also himself" (Prov. 11:24-25). That is, he who is generous to give and who gives to satisfy another's hunger, will experience such generosity of God upon him.

And in Isaiah: "Is it not to deal thy bread to the hungry, and that thou bring the poor that are cast out to thy house? when thou seest the naked, that thou cover him; and that thou hide not thyself from thine own flesh? . . . And if thou draw out thy soul to the hungry, and satisfy the afflicted soul; . . . thou shalt be like a watered garden, and like a spring of water, whose waters fail not" (Isa. 58:7-11).

And Paul affirms what is written in Psalms: "As it is written, He hath dispersed abroad; He hath given to the poor: His righteousness remaineth for ever. Now He that ministereth seed to the sower [will also] minister bread for your food" (2 Cor. 9:9-10; Ps. 112:9).

TIMOTHY: This is a good manner of lending with interest.

DANIEL: This is a manner of lending which is not forbidden by God, but instead is strongly commanded and required of all by Him. But there are few to be found who desire to be lenders in this way, seeing that there are few who place any faith in the promise of God or who are as assured of receiving from Him what He has promised than they are of receiving from men what they are required to repay them. All this evil proceeds from the fact that they are afraid of falling into poverty and of dying of hunger if they trust in God and act as He has commanded them. For they cannot believe that this manner of obtaining riches which God shows them by His promises and which the Spirit of God sets forth to them will actually work.

CHAPTER ELEVEN

A Closer Look at Usury

THE TRUE MEANING OF "USURY," AND THE DIFFERENCE BETWEEN IT AND "FŒNERATION," AND THE EQUITY WITHIN TRUE USURY

TIMOTHY: You have hit the mark. But I would still like to learn from you if all types of lending with interest are wholly forbidden by God among Christians, and whether there are any types that are lawful for them besides what you just mentioned.

DANIEL: Though this name usury is generally taken, according to the common manner of speaking, for all types of loans from which we receive some gain and profit above the principal, yet there is one type to which this name is more suitable than any other, which is called more properly by the jurists "fœneration,"[1] to distinguish it from the first.

TIMOTHY: Tell me then the difference which exists between the two of them.

DANIEL: Because it would be too lengthy if we desired to discuss it in depth and fully, I will only speak in general and as briefly as possible on as much as I think to be applicable to the matter we are dealing with.

Thus I consider usury to be the cost or price of the use of the principal, in accordance with the creditor's loss—that

[1] "*Fœneration,* lending out money at interest; the act of putting out money to usury." Henry Campbell Black, Black's Law Dictionary (West Publishing Company, St. Paul, Minn., 1968).

is, what the creditor receives as recompense for the damage or loss he might sustain because his principal is held by and in the possession of the debtor. This type of lending truly finds its foundation in the love which must rule the life of every man, for if love requires you to assist and show kindness to your neighbor, it also requires your neighbor to be considerate of the damage you receive and the danger in which you place yourself so that he might have goods and profit from the kindness and service you render him. For it is not reasonable for the debtor to profit from the loss of the creditor. Therefore the laws provided for this when they set a reasonable interest rate which the debtor is bound to pay to the lender as a recompense for the loss and interest which the creditor could have for lack of his goods which are in another's hands, which will profit him as much as if his goods were in his own hands, to serve himself with, just as he who possesses it is served by it. For in this way a rule is made for the creditor in order that he might not ask a larger repayment than what is just and reasonable. It is made for the debtor also, in order that he might not, by his ingratitude and wickedness, withhold the repayment due to the lender.

TIMOTHY: From what I can understand from your words, you do not approve of any type of usury except when some type of repayment above the principal amount is given as a recompense for the risk to which the lender is exposed, or for the loss which he receives from lending his money or goods, from which he could receive benefit if he had kept them, and the benefit prevented by this means, which he might receive.

DANIEL: I understand it so.

TIMOTHY: It seems that we could also add to this manner of lending the type of revenues commonly called investments or loans given for a stipulated period of time.

DANIEL: There is some reason and justice for it, for he who lends money on condition that he will annually receive some particular amount of interest back by the laws relinquishes his money in such a way that it is not in his power to ask it back when he wants it except by losing the interest which is due him, but instead the money remains in the power of him who received it, who can give it to whomever he pleases or can keep it for himself, as long as he pays the interest.

THE OTHER TYPE OF USURY CALLED "FŒNERATION" OR "RENÈVE"

TIMOTHY: Seeing that it is so, tell me now about this type of usury which you have called fœneration.

DANIEL: It is when these conditions we have just set forth are not met, by which the money is loaned by the creditor, who only has regard for his own profit, and who leaves all the danger and disadvantage to the debtor without having any regard for his poverty or need. For, by doing this, he plucks fruit from an unproductive thing and from the labor of another, reaping without sowing, eating by the sweat and pain of others, and takes out of the hands and mouths of the poor, seeing that he adds nothing to his labor or to his industry and that he shares in neither his risk nor damage.

This manner of action is against the rule of humanity which obliges us to assist one another and to share in all dangers and damages in the things from which we hope to receive gain and profit. For it is not humanity to have a greater love for keeping your money idle in your coffers without assisting those who are in need when you have a good means of doing so, or of taking profit from them from this money which would only have remained idle in your hands if you had not loaned it to them.

Secondly, just as much as such a manner of living is not suitable to human society nor such gain suitable to our nature and the order which God has given to men, so the example is wicked and dangerous because of the thefts, robberies, extortions, and brigandage which can be committed under the cover and disguise of such business and such dealings. If you like, in order to place a difference between this and the other, we will call this type of usury by the name of *renève,* which is used in certain countries and which always bears a wicked meaning.

THE RULE OF A GOOD CONSCIENCE IN THESE MATTERS; AND THE USURY BY WHICH THE POOR ARE TRAMPLED UPON; AND WHAT A PLAGUE AND TEMPEST CRUEL AND UNLAWFUL USURY IS AMONG MEN

TIMOTHY: There are many replies which could be made against what you have just said, but this could not be done quickly if we desired to discuss all the reasons and allegations which could be alleged from each side concerning this matter. Therefore it seems to me that, following the foundations and reasons you have set forth, we can have no more suitable rule or more just law to instruct us what types of usury are lawful or unlawful for us, than our conscience.

DANIEL: It is true, if it is ruled by the Word of God as it ought to be. For the Word says: "If thy brother be waxen poor, and fallen in decay with thee; then thou shalt relieve him: yea, though he be a stranger, or a sojourner; that he may live with thee. Take thou no usury of him, or increase: but fear thy God; that thy brother may live with thee. Thou shalt not give him thy money upon usury, nor lend him thy victuals for increase," and: "Unto a stranger thou mayest lend upon usury; but unto thy brother thou shalt not lend upon usury: that the LORD thy God may bless thee in all that thou settest thine hand to in the land whither thou goest to possess it" (Lev. 25:35-37; Deut. 23:20).

There are many who dream up their own desires from their consciences, and always rule them according to their profit. Therefore, in order that we might better understand how usury (such as God forbids) is unsuitable for a just man, the Lord spoke by His prophet: "He that hath not given forth upon usury, neither hath taken any increase" will "abide in Thy tabernacle" and "dwell in Thy holy hill" (Eze. 18:8; Ps. 15:1, 5). Nehemiah likewise very strongly rebuked the cruelty of the creditors who, after the return from Babylon, crushed their poor brethren by usury (Neh. 5:1-13).

TIMOTHY: Experience clearly shows us that God did not so expressly forbid this without good and just reason. Therefore I am not at all surprised that the canonists judged usurers and extortionists so inhuman, worthy of public infamy, and unworthy of Christian communion or burial, and that their testaments were ratified among the other troubles to which they were also condemned besides the divine punishment prepared for them. For this is a scourge and a horrible tempest in human society, which endlessly sends men to beggary and extreme poverty, and is a crime of excessive cruelty which slits men's throats.

DANIEL: This is why they are not incorrect who compare them to wasps, leeches, tumors, and cancer. For there is no cancer so dangerous or savage beast so cruel as this beast called *usury*—or, if you prefer it, *fœneration* or *renève*—which for this reason is rightly called by the Hebrews *neshek,* which comes from a word meaning *to bite.* I mean this of the unlawful fœnerations and extortion we spoke of which are put into practice against all humanity and all charity.

Therefore it is written in Deuteronomy: "Thou shalt not lend upon usury to thy brother; usury of money, usury of victuals, usury of any thing that is lent upon usury: unto a stranger thou mayest lend upon usury; but unto thy brother thou shalt not lend upon usury: that the Lord thy God may bless thee in all that thou settest thine hand to in the land whither thou goest to possess it" (Deut. 23:19-20). The words which Moses uses in this passage rightly carry this meaning, though all do not translate it so. And by the name of brother he means those who are of the people of God and who follow the Word and the true religion found within it.

WHAT TYPE OF USURY GOD HAS PARTICULARLY FORBIDDEN IN HIS LAW; AND HOW IT IS NOT ENOUGH FOR A CHRISTIAN TO REFRAIN FROM LENDING HIS MONEY AT INTEREST TO THE POOR IF HE DOES NOT ALSO ASSIST THE POOR IN THEIR NEEDS

TIMOTHY: You have done well in stating this exception. For it seems by the manner of speaking which God used in the laws given against the types of usury you just mentioned, that He is concerned with those who work harm to their neighbor and who place him in poverty and consume his goods instead of assisting him. For, seeing that "love is the fulfillment of the law," it seems to me that usury which does not violate this, but to the contrary is profitable to men, must not be included in these laws.

DANIEL: You heard what I said previously. If we can truly keep the Law quoted by Jesus Christ to this purpose in the Gospels according to Matthew and Luke, we would have no more need of any further legislation regarding usury. "As ye would that men should do to you," He said, "do ye also to them likewise" (Luke 6:31; Mat. 7:12).

TIMOTHY: You speak the truth, but we still have a long way to go to attain this.

DANIEL: Therefore it is greatly to be feared that very few men can be trusted with a free rein in such a case, and that no matter what moderation and hindrance might be given to their covetousness and insatiable greed, yet they will always proceed beyond measure.

And secondly, we must also understand that it is not enough for us to beware of giving our money at usury to the poor people who are in need, but we must also labor to assist them as we are able. I say this because there are some who, in order to avoid this label of *usurer* and *extortioner*, refuse to lend their money at profit in the manner in which it is commonly given by usury. But, because they also do not desire to lend without receiving some profit, they keep their money without using it to serve or assist anyone despite the fact that they could easily lend it without harm to themselves.

TIMOTHY: I have heard of such men, and I did not know what to say of them or how I could think of them any more highly than the usurers. There is a difference between them in the fact that they harm their brethren in a different manner than the others, but both of them certainly cause much damage and harm. The one side does it by not doing the good which they ought to do, and the others by doing evil and causing damage instead of assisting and helping. But what do you say of those who declare themselves to be "of the Church" and who forbid others from lending at usury, but who make an exception for themselves?

DANIEL: You can judge this (and also their love) by what we have already said on this matter.

TIMOTHY: What a beautiful charity of the Holy Mother Church!

THE JUDGMENT AND VENGEANCE OF GOD EXECUTED UPON MEN BY MEANS OF USURY, TO CORRECT THEIR PRIDE AND DISHONESTY AND THEIR VANITIES AND EXTRAVAGANCE

DANIEL: Therefore when we see this, we must recognize (as we already mentioned previously) that this is an evil and a curse sent upon men by the wrath of God (just as the other curses with which He threatens the transgressors of His Law) to punish their iniquities, giving them on the one hand greedy and inhuman men who would rather watch their brethren perish before lending them a single penny in their dire need, and on the other hand usurers as executioners. And therefore it is expressly said that the wicked who are pursued by the curse of God will be forced to borrow in their own time of need, and it will be lent to them with usury (Ps. 37:21; Deut. 28:43-44). For it is very reasonable that the pride and unfaithfulness of men should be chastised by such scourges. For there is such vast dishonesty in many that they keep neither faith nor word, and they give nothing but annoyance and insult for the kindness and services rendered to them. Therefore their ingratitude and dishonesty does not give occasion for someone to lend to and aid them at another time, but instead they deserve rather to be left without aid or assistance.

There are also others who seek to live in idleness without doing anything except consuming and borrowing, and others who can never be reckless enough and are never concerned about anything besides spending money on their fine clothing, luxuries, and sensual pleasures, without concerning themselves with whether their goods will be sufficient or not for the expenses they daily make. But after they have fallen into the hands of the moneylenders, they are forced to learn lessons which they are not accustomed to. They can then say that they have fallen into the hands of those who rob them blind. But the worst is that they still cannot recognize the hand of God upon them, but instead they grow angry in themselves and do not consider the One who holds the rod by which they are chastised.

TIMOTHY: You make me think of something I had not considered so deeply before. I have often been astonished at many rich and wealthy houses which I have seen melt away before my eyes in a very little time, just as snow melts before the sun and wax before the fire [Ps. 68:2]. But I am no longer surprised after I have considered your train of thought and the follies and luxuries on which they have expended their wealth. For them, such reformations and reformers are needed to remedy such excess and such vanities.

DANIEL: You must note that God often punishes usurers even by other usurers, just as He punishes thieves, looters, and robbers by others like them. For, after they have filled their houses and enriched their children by spoiling others and by ill-gotten gain, they find others similar to themselves who do the same to them. Also, if it were a question of specifying the different types of usuries which exist today among men and the horrible crimes which are committed by that means, and to set forth examples of those who have been destroyed by it, there would be none who would not be greatly horrified at the retelling of it.

CHAPTER TWELVE

Lawsuits and Lawyers

THOSE WHO CUNNINGLY GO TO COURT TO DECEIVE THEIR NEIGHBOR AND TO OBTAIN OR KEEP WHAT BELONGS TO OTHERS

TIMOTHY: Let us now leave usurers with their usury for the thieves and highway robbers that they are, and pursue the rest of the matters pertaining to the exposition of this commandment. Thus let us now speak of the other types of deception by which we rob our neighbors.

DANIEL: We could truly still place among thieves who rob by guile and deception all those litigants who never go to court except to obtain what belongs to others or to demand what is not due them, hoping to be able to outwit their opponents by deceit and underhanded dealings, or hoping to find a way to escape paying their debts or to delay the payment of them. They meanwhile enjoy the possessions of another while harming their neighbor, and attempt to outwit their creditors by deceitful process at law, in order to make the creditors lose what is rightfully theirs. For, if there are prosecutors who without reason demand what is not justly due them, there are even more defendants who deny what they owe. And, among these, many find a means of retaining the rights and titles of their opponents in order to disarm them judicially so that they cannot uphold or defend their lawful rights.

TIMOTHY: You haven't even mentioned those who sometimes (for very little sums of money which are due them) remove by law the possessions of those who are indebted to them, even though their possessions are worth two or three times the value of what is due them. And then they foreclose on them when they miss a payment, in such a way that many have often obtained all the possessions of many poor debtors for no more than a crust of bread. And, to better achieve their designs, they take them to court when they see them most burdened and least able to satisfy their creditors. Doesn't it seem that such practices are truly worthy of being included among the thefts committed by guile and deception?

DANIEL: They not only deserve to be called thefts, but also larcenies, highway robberies, and extortions.

TIMOTHY: But they respond that they have obtained by justice and by lawful means what they have stolen in this manner, and that they have been given it by sentence of the judge. What then can be said when they unjustly possess such goods?

DANIEL: It truly appears that there is no longer any justice or right in the world, seeing that true justice has passed away. But, far from this guise covering their robberies and crimes, to the contrary it intensifies their thefts, and renders them as guilty and much more execrable than any sacrilege which might be committed.

For, firstly, they steal as much as they have received beyond what is due them.

Secondly, the expense which they cause the poor people to incur by devouring and consuming their money in legal fees is still another type of theft by which they oppress them, seeing that they are the cause of such expense. For how many times does it happen that the court costs exceed the value of the possessions being disputed?

Thirdly, if it is considered sacrilege when someone steals sacred things from sacred places, why wouldn't these also be taken for such—indeed for cutthroats and the most despicable criminals—who steal the goods of another in the sacred place of the majesty of God where He has established the seat of His justice? If a servant stole something in his master's house, his act would be called theft. And because he is a member of the household, he will be judged worthy of a much greater punishment than if the crime had been committed by another, or in another house. And if someone stole something in the house of a king or a ruler—indeed, in his very bedchamber—how would this thief be treated?

TIMOTHY: It is easy to judge. For he would be regarded as a desecrator of the house of the king and ruler.

DANIEL: Thus you can clearly imagine how God will treat these thieves who make His house—which is the house and seat of justice—a den of thieves and criminals.

MAGISTRATES AND OFFICERS WHO ENCOURAGE SUCH DECEIVERS AND THIEVES IN THE COURTS OF JUSTICE, AND FAVOR INSTEAD OF HINDERING THEM; AND THE PUNISHMENT OF GOD UPON MEN WHEN HE GIVES THEM SUCH OFFICIALS, AND THE REASON FOR IT

TIMOTHY: If these are thieves, the judges, magistrates, prosecutors, attorneys, superintendents, secretaries, and all officers who, being corrupt and being aware of such deceptions, encourage the iniquity and wickedness of such people, how should these men be regarded?

DANIEL: Isaiah gives the answer to your question when he says: "Thy princes are rebellious, and companions of thieves: every one loveth gifts, and followeth after rewards: they judge not the fatherless, neither doth the cause of the widow come unto them" (Isa. 1:23). He likewise condemns those who "justify the wicked for reward, and take away the righteousness of the righteous from him" (Isa. 5:23). In this way they are also often murderers.

TIMOTHY: There are today vast legal battles among men because of such corruptions.

DANIEL: The reason for it is very just, indeed. But those who battle them in court must also beware that they themselves are not the cause of their own misfortune and of that of others. For few are found who have any great desire to see justice upheld toward their neighbor. But, in order to do him wrong, every man endeavors to bribe those from whom they hope to receive assistance and service in order that they might win their suit.

And, just as one person labors on the one side to deceive his opponent, so the other person labors in the same way on the other side. And by this God punishes us by one another, and measures back to us with the same measure we used with others (Mat. 7:2). For, as we endeavor to win the favor of the officials in order that they might uphold our cause, our adversaries are doing just as much on their side. And, because by this we have accustomed these officials to expect such gifts, it is very difficult afterward to be received by them unless we bring them something. And if the opposing party gives them even more than we do, we will be in great danger of losing everything, no matter how just a cause we might have. Thus, if we are plundered and robbed in this manner, we deserve it. For we ourselves have created the tyrants and thieves who plunder and tyrannize over us. Therefore it is more than reasonable for us to receive the wages which are due us.

THE DUTY OF LAWYERS AND OFFICIALS WHO ARE EMPLOYED BY THOSE WHO REPRESENT AN EVIL CAUSE IN JUSTICE

TIMOTHY: This punishment is very just. But, following what we said regarding the abetting of those who have an evil cause by those who ought to reject it, I have a doubt on which I would like your opinion: a man comes to me who has a wicked cause. He would like me to become his attorney or lawyer, and asks the court that I be assigned to him to seek to uphold his case. If I know that the cause is wicked, what should I do? If I were at liberty, I know very well what I would do; I would tell him frankly what I thought, and then if he did not wish to drop the case, following my advice, I would tell him to seek another counselor or attorney or lawyer other than myself. But if I were employed by the court or council and I was commanded to do it, what should I do? For if I refuse to do what I have been enjoined to by a court order, another might refuse just as I did, and in the same way. Or, if he takes the case, I would in some way condemn him by my prejudice, as if he had less conscience than I did in taking on a wicked case.

Secondly, it seems that by this same means I would attribute to myself the office of judge (who judges the case according to his own opinion) before it has been debated in court.

And if I took on the case, considering it to be wicked, how could I do it in good conscience? For it might happen that I would become the reason why he who did the wrong wins his case against the man who had the most right on his side.

DANIEL: This must be determined on a case-by-case basis. Some cases are more obviously wicked than others. Thus we might be deceived in our own judgment, and might judge a good case to be wicked because of our lack of properly understanding it. Therefore we must not quickly pass judgment on others.

Secondly, there is a difference between the attorney and the judge. When you are appointed as an attorney in a particular case, it is proper for you to set forth what the party for whom you speak desires to be put forth, in order that it might be debated in court so that it can be judged by those who are appointed to that task. If the party demands of you more than can be demanded of a just man, you must know your duty.

If you are appointed to give your advice as a counselor or judge, you must speak according to your conscience, and do all which must be done according to your office in order that no wrong be done to anyone, and that you do not partake in the thefts and iniquities of others.

CHAPTER THIRTEEN

Gambling and Illegitimate Occupations

GAMBLING, AND THE THEFTS COMMITTED IN IT

TIMOTHY: I am content concerning this point. What now would you say of gamblers who win money from others by playing games?

DANIEL: Can you doubt the fact that these are also very clearly thieves? For if a game is played to win money, what else can it be except a means to deceive and steal from another? For even though he who loses his money was truly attempting to win his companion's money, and though he willingly engaged in the gambling with this hope in mind, yet, seeing that he who won the money did not win it by doing anything which might benefit him to whom the money belongs, he cannot possess or keep it except as a trickster and a thief. There is no difference between him and a common thief except in the fact that these thieves enjoy greater privileges and have much greater pretenses of avoiding the name of thief among men than do the others.

Secondly, isn't there a grievous theft committed against the time which is lost in gaming, if they are not profitable games which might serve either for the health of the body or for some other endeavor profitable to the country, as are the games of archery, crossbow, and the like? (I won't even begin to mention the oaths, denials of God, and blasphemies which are there committed against the third commandment.)

Also, how many players of games are thieves of another sort as well? For some begin to steal in order to cover the cost of the games they are addicted to. And others, after they have played and lost all their money and possessions at these games, must find another means of obtaining more, and do not do it by any just labor, but by theft. For they cannot employ the time in labor and work which they employ in games and idleness. Nor can they feed their families in such a way.

TIMOTHY: What you say concerns the poor, but it is not the same with kings, rulers, great lords, rich men and wealthy women, and ladies and their daughters, among whom many make this an occupation as well as the men.

DANIEL: Won't all these which you mention also be required to give an account of their lost time which could have been employed in better things? Have they nothing better to employ themselves with?

TIMOTHY: But who more than them ought to be as concerned with saving, and who else has more to lose than they do, considering the charge committed to them, if they desire to fulfill it as they ought, both towards God and men?

DANIEL: And are the wickednesses which they commit in gaming any more lawful than those of the others? And though they have a greater abundance of goods than the poor, yet they must still consider what they have and the fact that they will give an account of it. Shouldn't they consider why it was placed in their hands and whether they are employing it as they ought to be employing it? Furthermore, do they not play at the expense of the poor, whom they force to pay for the games and the debauched pleasures they engage in?

TIMOTHY: The poor people of whom you speak can truly testify to this. But tell me if you find any difference at all between gambling and betting, which many make an occupation of just like gambling, and often win or lose vast sums of money by it, just as in gambling.

DANIEL: I see no difference between them except that it is a different type of trickery and theft very closely related to gambling.

THOSE WHO LEND SPACE TO GAMBLERS AND WHO PROFIT FROM THEM, AND THOSE WHO MAKE OR SELL THE INSTRUMENTS NECESSARY FOR SUCH GAMES

TIMOTHY: If I am correct in my thinking, those who lease a place to gamblers (as hotels, bars, and other similar places) are thus the same as a receiver of stolen goods who profits from a swindler or a thief; and particularly those who encourage debauched young people to do this, who often steal from their fathers and mothers in order to have enough money for their gambling, and by doing this they enter upon the road which will lead them to the scaffold.

DANIEL: You must not doubt it. For if the gamblers are thieves, those who receive profit from them and who provide them the means to gamble are even more so, for without them they could not do what they do (Prov. 28:10). They are just the same as brothel-keepers in this regard.

TIMOTHY: Thus, in my opinion, we must say the same of those who make the cards, dice, and other such instruments to serve for unlawful gaming.

DANIEL: They could in the first place defend themselves by saying that it is not their duty to inquire or be concerned about what someone might do with their merchandise, or to ask an account of those who buy them. Otherwise they could never sell anything, for many will abuse it, no matter what it is. According to this line of reasoning, we must not make firearms because criminals will use them to kill people.

Besides this they will say that someone can use their

merchandise as a pastime without losing his money, and that they sell them for no other reason than that.

But when all is said and done, it would be much more honest for them to devote themselves to other trades and occupations than these, seeing that such great evil can proceed from the use of such merchandise, and no good can come of it. Or, if any good does come from it, it is very difficult for this to occur, and the good is so small that it is almost impossible to discover it. Therefore this is not the same as with firearms, which can be used as a defense of one's possessions and country and as other things which are useful and necessary for the life of men. I understand this of games which serve to no public good or to any good or profitable exercise either for the body or the spirit of man, as are card games and dicing and other similar things.

THOSE WHO MAKE MERCHANDISE OF THE INSTRUMENTS OF IDOLATRY, AND THE EXCUSES THEY SET FORTH TO COVER THEIR DEEDS

TIMOTHY: We can say the same of those who sell images, rosaries, wax tapers, lights, candles, and other such instruments of idolatry for idolaters to use in their worship; and of all those who employ themselves in seducing people in order to take money from them, particularly the false prophets and ministers of the antichrist.

DANIEL: This is worse than theft, because the name of God is so villainously dishonored by idolatry (as we already discussed in its place), and because these people assist, approve of, and further such abominations by what they do. For, if the accomplices in some wicked crime who assist those who commit it are considered guilty of the same crime, why would these people here be exempt, seeing that they hold their own profit in much greater esteem than the honor and glory of God? (Rom. 1:23.)

TIMOTHY: They will again reply with what we just said of the merchandise made and sold for games, and declare that their occupation is not so useless, but can indeed serve very well for many good things.

DANIEL: Let them tell me then to what good use the idols made to represent God and the saints can be put, and the rosaries as well, and all the other things. What can they be used for besides idolatry?

There is some greater pretense for the candles and wax tapers, because they can be used to serve other purposes than idolatry. But if you are laboring in some occupation and your work is being deliberately misused by some, and you know it very well, is it not the same as if you sold poison to an assassin so that he could poison someone? Or if you sold a sword to a criminal so that he could kill people? Would you be innocent of the crimes committed by such people in such a case? You know very well that no one dares to sell poison indiscriminately, even though it might be useful for more things than simply to poison people. What then of the merchandise that serves no other purpose than poison?

TIMOTHY: They will still reply that if they do not do it, it will not remain undone, for other men will be found to take up their occupation.

DANIEL: Their reasoning is about as good as if a brothel-keeper said that another man would run his establishment if he didn't do it. But it doesn't follow that, just because others desire to labor against their duty, you must follow their example. You will not be required to give an answer to God for their deeds, but for yours alone (Rom. 14:12).

OCCUPATIONS AND MERCHANDISE, AND PROFESSIONS WHICH ARE HARMFUL, OR AT LEAST USELESS, FOR MANKIND

TIMOTHY: Seeing that you have stumbled upon the topic of brothel-keepers, I think that we could truly say the same not only of the profit which they and the madams receive from the prostitutes and pimps who serve them, but also of those who employ themselves in any job or occupation outside of the lawful calling of God, by which God is dishonored or our neighbor is harmed, and from which no benefit can come either to the church of God or to the country.

DANIEL: It is quite true, for if this is not done, the calling is not of God, and the occupation is not a means ordained by Him to earn our daily bread. Thus we do not eat our own bread and do not receive it from God's hand, but instead we eat the bread of others and receive it as though it came directly from the devil's hand; for we cannot boast that we have obeyed God's commandment, by which He declared to man that he must eat bread by the sweat of his brow (Gen. 3:19). Thus it is not enough for us to eat our bread with labor and grand travail, but this labor and travail must also be directed to an honest end which serves to the glory of God and the benefit of our neighbor.

For many earn their living with great labor and pain in wicked and unlawful practices; highway robbers undergo great labor and danger, but they cannot pride themselves in this at all or think that by this means they have fulfilled God's commandment. On this you must note that all those who live and profit from such occupations and who give themselves to wicked practices and deceive and steal, are mocking God when they ask of Him their daily bread. For, by asking Him for it, they testify that He can give it to them and desires to give it to them, and that they wish to receive it from no other hand than His, as children from the hand of their father; otherwise they would not ask it of Him. Yet after they have made this prayer, they run off to the devil and request it from his hand, taking the path which they take to seek it from him. By this they disown God as their Father and Provider, and take the devil instead of Him.

TIMOTHY: Thus it follows, seeing that it is as you say, that all those who violate this commandment given against stealing also violate this petition of our Lord in which we ask God for our daily bread.

DANIEL: That is very clear.

CHAPTER FOURTEEN

Robbing the Poor by Unjust Charity

THOSE WHO PREY ON WILLS AND LEGACIES; AND THOSE WHO USE BRIBERY TO APPROPRIATE TO THEMSELVES THE GOODS OF ANOTHER

TIMOTHY: I agree with you. But what then do you say of those who by flatteries, enticing speech, and other cunning means, induce others to give them their possessions and inheritance, either by donations or by legacies or some other similar means, thus defrauding those to whom it belongs by right?

DANIEL: We must not doubt that these also must be placed among the rank of thieves, among whom priests and monks have above all others strongly played the part. For, through their false doctrine and their lies and attractive words, they have gathered to themselves the vast majority of men's possessions; so much so that the true heirs themselves have been defrauded. Indeed, even the children have been deprived of the possessions and inheritances of their fathers and mothers!

THOSE WHO LIVE ON CHARITY WITHOUT NEEDING IT; AND THE ROBBING OF THE TRULY POOR WHICH IS COMMITTED BY THIS MEANS, AND PARTICULARLY BY THE MONKS

TIMOTHY: Many can testify to this. It also seems to me that those who ask for charity and alms without really needing it, and who live by begging when they have the means to make a living another way, must be taken for thieves because, through the deception and wickedness of their feigned poverty, they steal the charity which ought to be given to others who have a much greater need than they do. For I can assure you that I have known men who, still possessing an abundance of money in their wallets, beg alms from the poor, and make them give to many when they themselves possess more money and goods than many of them do.

But I dislike more than anything else this manner of living which exists in many of those who boast themselves of the knowledge of the truth of the Gospel, and who have left their country and possessions to follow it, and particularly a pile of monks more defrocked than unmonked, who are always taking up an offering. For, because such persons have always been accustomed to take and receive and never to give, they know no other occupation than to beg, take up an offering, ask, and receive. As soon as there is no one to collect or receive from, it seems to them as if the earth must fail them, and they live in great agitation until they have money in their wallet, because they watch it diminish rather than grow. Therefore they must take up an offering before they see the end.

DANIEL: There can be no doubt that all these are nothing more than true imposters and swindlers. For if we consider as thieves all those who by their miserliness and stinginess leave the poor to suffer without having any compassion on them and without assisting them by charity in their time of need, these here have an even greater reason to be considered thieves who pressure their neighbors and the Church without just cause, and who make them give to them what is due to others by the commandment of God. For it is nearly the same with these men as if you requested and demanded payment for a debt which belonged to another, taking by this means what is due him, or being the reason why he must pay two debts, though he only owed one.

TIMOTHY: I strongly fear in this case that all four orders of monks, and all like them (both monks and nuns), are nothing more than orders of thieves—indeed, very great thieves, for they are grand rascals, devouring the substance with which many genuinely poor people could be greatly relieved.

DANIEL: It is very true, for if we have good reason to call people thieves who, having become poor by their own fault through their laziness, negligence, idleness, gluttony, drunkenness, and other similar vices and excesses, take the alms from those who are truly poor—to whom they are rightly due—how much greater reason have we to consider as thieves all these lazy bellies who live in idleness off of the charity due to the Church and the poor? By this they are not only thieves, but are also truly guilty of sacrilege.

THOSE WHO KNOWINGLY RETAIN THE DEBTS OF THEIR CREDITORS IF THEIR CREDITORS DO NOT POSSESS THE MEANS TO BRING THEM TO JUSTICE

TIMOTHY: Seeing that you mentioned debts, I ask you on this head what you think of those who are indebted to someone and who know it well, and yet if their creditor forgets the debt or if he loses the contract and the agreement or titles by which it can be proved that the debt is owed, or if the debtor can find some way to steal or take them so that his creditor cannot claim it, and, if he holds the debt in his possession under the hope that the creditor has been deprived of his rights by which he could constrain him to act justly, isn't such a person a true thief?

DANIEL: He is so no less than if he had snatched his creditor's wallet or if he had stolen his money out of it.

FORGERS WHO CREATE FALSE DOCUMENTS; AND THOSE WHO MOVE THE BOUNDARY MARKERS OF THEIR NEIGHBORS' PROPERTY

TIMOTHY: And aren't forgers who make false documents part of the same band of thieves?

DANIEL: They are even worse—indeed, if I dare say it—than

the counterfeiters of false money and highway robbers. For, by a single stroke of the pen, they can make a man lose all his property and everything he owns, and slit his throat like a robber, and overturn all right and justice.

TIMOTHY: We have still not spoken of those who move the boundary markers of their neighbors' lands and properties.

DANIEL: God openly speaks against them in His Law. And, in order that we might better understand how displeasing such iniquity is to Him (by which great disorder and confusion are also introduced into human society), He has decreed a most express curse against these people among those curses which He gives against the transgressors of His Law, and not without reason. For such types of theft create great havoc among men and the public order, and are often the cause of vast wars and controversies. Therefore He says: "Cursed be he that removeth his neighbour's landmark." And all the people will say: "So let it be" (Deut. 27:17).

UNLAWFUL TRADES AND OCCUPATIONS, AND THE THINGS NECESSARY IN ALL TRADES AND OCCUPATIONS TO BE ABLE TO PROFIT FROM THEM ACCORDING TO GOD AND WITHOUT THEFT

TIMOTHY: From what I can understand by all this discussion that we have had, we must firstly consider as theft all profit that we gain by any trade, practice, and occupation not ordained by God.

Secondly, we must consider as such not only all occupations that clearly cause harm to our neighbor, but also all those which in no way serve to advance the honor of God and the edification of the Church, and which profit neither the public good nor any person whatever.

Thirdly, it is not enough for the trades and occupations we engage in to be lawful; but we must also use them in a lawful manner, and not abuse them in any way. For, if we do abuse them, we make a trade or occupation evil even though it might be good and lawful by nature. By doing this we are no better than those who engage in unlawful trades and occupations, but are much worse because we employ the commandment of God to cover ourselves in order that we might engage in and disguise our thefts. For this reason I would still like you to make some mention of this matter according to the positions, trades, and occupations which are most common among men, in order that I might better understand how we ought to conduct ourselves in order to avoid the crime of theft, and how we can be a thief by not discharging our office as we ought.

DANIEL: I am happy to do so.

CHAPTER FIFTEEN

Thefts Committed in the Ministry of the Church

PRELATES AND MINISTERS OF THE PAPAL CHURCH, AND THE CAUSES AND REASONS WHY THEY (AND THOSE WHO SHARE IN THEIR PLUNDER WITH THEM) ARE ALL THIEVES, SACRILEGIOUS PERSONS, AND SIMONIACS[1]

TIMOTHY: Let us then begin with those who ought to be "the light of the world" and who ought, by true doctrine and good example, to teach others to follow the rule and commandments of God (Mat. 5:14). Thus we will firstly begin with the popes and ministers of the church.

DANIEL: We would have matter enough to deal with here if we desired to discuss it in detail, but it will be sufficient if we simply touch upon it in general. For the first, we must note that as there are two types of church, so there are also two types of pastors and ministers. Now, as the church of the antichrist robs from and steals what belongs to Jesus Christ's Church, so also all the ministers of this church of the antichrist—from the greatest to the least—can be no more than true thieves and workers of sacrilege, stealing for themselves the goods which are due to the true ministers of Jesus Christ's Church and its poor members (as we already discussed previously when speaking of monks and mendicants). For, as they falsely usurp the place of the true pastors and ministers of the Church without fulfilling the office

[1] Simoniac – one who engages in spiritual matters or duties for monetary profit. The name is derived from Simon Magus (Acts 8:18-19).

enjoined to them, so likewise under false titles they usurp the goods which are ordained for the preservation of the ministry of the Church and for the relief of the poor.

TIMOTHY: Thus in this case there is today neither pope, cardinal, bishop, priest, monk, nor any man whatever who profits from the papal church, who is not a thief and a sacrilegious man, not only of the Word of God which they steal from the people (as you already discussed previously), but also of earthly possessions. And not only are they thieves, but so also are all their relatives and friends who receive any gain or profit from them and are enriched by them.

DANIEL: It is doubtless true. And just as much as each of them possesses more and is elevated to a higher position, he is that much greater a thief and a sacrilegious man, and a greater leader among his companions. Also, even if their state and office to which they say they are called was ordained by God, yet according to their own decrees and canons there would be few among them who would not be simoniacs, because there are none who have not bought and sold the benefices[2] which they enjoy and the offices and sacraments with which they boast of being ministers, and of which they daily make merchandise. By doing this they render themselves fully subject to the curse given to Simon the Magician by Peter, from whom the name simony is taken (Acts 8:18-23).

Furthermore, besides the fact that their position is not received from God and that they have not arrived at it by the steps and means set forth even in their canons themselves, there is still this point, that the vast majority of them do not even do the work to which they claim to be called, despite the fact that it costs them nothing at all.

Now, if a servant or a laborer received wages for a service or a work which he did not do, he must be considered a thief. Why then aren't these men considered such who not only take the wages due to the true ministers of the Church (under the title of the ministry which these false pastors do not fulfill at

[2] Benefice – revenue received from the church.

all), but even more, a single one of them often takes from the revenues enough to nourish the ministers and the poor of an entire country? Therefore if the servant and workman must be considered thieves who are paid for a service and labor which they did not do, how much more ought we to consider him an even worse thief who is paid, not only when he has not done the service for which he receives wages, but besides this when he has also done great damage to his master?

THE WAGES ORDAINED BY GOD FOR THE TRUE MINISTERS OF THE CHURCH, AND THOSE WHO WITHHOLD THEM; AND THE THEFT OF THE MINISTERS WHO TAKE THE PLACE OF MERCENARIES IN THE CHURCH INSTEAD OF TRUE PASTORS

TIMOTHY: Thus you desire to conclude that all those who bear the name of pastors and ministers of the Church are thieves and sacrilegious men except those who, following the example of the apostles and true bishops, pastors, and ministers of the ancient Church, serve in the ministry of the Gospel.

DANIEL: The commandment which God made for the Levites in the church of Israel for the preservation of its ministry, and the one also that Paul mentioned concerning the wages due to the ministers of the Gospel, clearly show this. For, when it is said: "The labourer is worthy of his reward," and "they which preach the gospel should live of the gospel," and that those who acquit themselves well of their office are "worthy of double honour," it is easy to understand by the contrary that those who are not such are also not worthy of such things (1 Tim. 5:17-18; 1 Cor. 9:14; Mat. 10:9-10; Luke 10:7).

TIMOTHY: If true ministers are worthy of their wages, it also follows that those whom they serve are not only thieves, but are also guilty of sacrilege if they do not give them the wages which are due them. For, if a man is a thief when he withholds the salary which is justly due to his servant, how much more must he be considered one who withholds what he ought to give to those who are not only his servants, but also like his fathers?

DANIEL: This is the same as if the child refused to provide for and assist his own father, as you can understand by what we have dealt with concerning the fifth commandment. For this reason our Lord Jesus commanded His disciples and apostles to lodge among those who were shown to be "children of peace" by receiving them and their teaching and by providing for them out of the goods within their house. By this He clearly shows that, just as Paul testified, "Let him that is taught in the word communicate unto him that teacheth in all good things" (Gal. 6:6; Mat. 10:11; Luke 10:5-7). For they show themselves more than unworthy of spiritual possessions who love their earthly goods too dearly to be deprived of them by sharing some portion of their earthly possessions in order to be participants in their spiritual.

TIMOTHY: If these people are such as you say, what must we think of those who are so unwilling to give any of their possessions for the preservation of the ministry of the Church that they even steal what has already been given to her for the purpose of the nourishment of her true ministers and the poor?

DANIEL: I leave you to consider it. But you must also note that if the pastors and ministers who boast themselves of the Gospel do not fulfill their duty with all diligence and faithfulness, they steal the wages which they receive just as much as unfaithful, dishonest, or idle servants who do not faithfully execute the labor for which they receive wages.

TIMOTHY: It is only right that every man must complete the work for which he desires to be paid or rewarded.

DANIEL: Yet there are some who so slightly acquit themselves of their duty that they never give much thought to the betterment of their flock as long as they can have the wool and the money.

TIMOTHY: These are not shepherds, but mercenaries. I am

acquainted with some who think they have fully acquitted themselves if they preach a sermon or two a week—indeed, even if it is a very meager one and contains precious little edification. To visit their flock in general, and particularly the sick, and to keep watch over the wayward, and to keep them from falling and bring them back to the right way, never concerns them in the least.

DANIEL: How I wish that what you say were not so true!

THOSE WHO KNOW THE TRUTH OF THE GOSPEL AND YET STILL RECEIVE BENEFICES FROM THE PAPISTS AND MAINTAIN THEIR OFFICE AS PAPAL MINISTERS

TIMOTHY: Let us leave these, and give me your opinion of certain other people who, though they know the truth, yet still retain the benefices which they at some point obtained from the papal church, remaining in their original position. They do this under the cover either that they sometimes preach and give alms, or that they in some sort fulfill the office of pastor more than the others who are fully papists and adversaries of the Gospel. Therefore they conclude that it is much better for them to be there rather than the others who do not fulfill as much of their duty and office as these, but to the contrary who wholly exploit the goods of the Church for their own sensual pleasures, and persecute the faithful.

DANIEL: At first glance they seem to have some foundation for what they say, and a very good appearance. But if we examine the thing a little more closely we will find many faults, both very dangerous and in much greater number than it seems to those who willingly deceive themselves in such a matter by their own reason, making themselves believe what they want to believe. I confess that they reason in one regard truly, that he who abuses his office and duty the least is, I do not say better (for all is worth nothing), but at least less wicked and the lesser thief. But there are other things to consider.

The first is that the good shepherd must be prepared (if

the need arises) to give his life for his sheep in order to fulfill his charge, rather than abandon them in order that he might get along well with the wolves. Now these treat the office of a pastor in this way, for they are very careful, as much as they can be, of saying and doing anything which might displease the wolves. They do not say or do anything except what they can say or do without placing themselves in any danger—or at least without placing themselves in any danger which they greatly fear.

By doing this they are firstly thieves of the Word of God because they hide it from the people and do not preach it in its purity and entirety, and because they do not provide sufficient pasture for the sheep who have been given to them to feed and provide for (1 Pet. 5:2). Thus it follows that they are also thieves of the wages they receive because they do not fully complete the work which they expect to be paid for. For the Prince of shepherds, who forbids them to add to His Word, also forbids them to leave anything out of it (Deut. 12:32).

Furthermore, instead of leading the people to the true knowledge and true worship of God, they maintain them in error and idolatry both by their wicked example and because they fail to give them sufficient and complete teaching. For, not content with concealing the Word of God which they ought to preach fully and not only out of one side of their mouth, besides this they do the very thing they condemn, or which they ought to condemn themselves for, and this is done either by themselves fulfilling the papal positions contrary to the teaching of God, or by substituting others to fulfill it in their name. By this they destroy as much and more than they build by making an open profession of superstition and idolatry and by maintaining the people in it by their deceit and hypocrisy, which they are bound to remove themselves from—indeed, even at the risk of their own life.

Or, if they cannot execute the true office of pastors because they are prevented by the enemies of the truth, they ought to leave their office in order to declare by this that they condemn this diabolical state. For, in doing this, they would live sermons which would perhaps bring much greater edification than all the sermons they preached the entire time they remained in such a state. For it is an excellent sermon which shows by effect and deed that one much more dearly prefers to renounce the feasting of the antichrist and its rich foods and to forsake all (following the example of Jacob) to inherit the blessing of God rather than abandon Jesus Christ "as Esau, who for one morsel of meat sold his birthright," and lose their eternal inheritance and the blessing of our heavenly Father (Heb. 12:16; Gen. 25:29-35).

THE EXCUSES THESE MEN SET FORTH CONCERNING THE GOOD WHICH THEY DO BY REMAINING IN THEIR PRESENT STATE

TIMOTHY: But they say that they are not abandoning Him, and that worse men will come in their place, and that they do what they can for the comfort of the believers, and that they give alms, which others would not do.

DANIEL: They fear that if they are not Satan's brothel-keepers, employed by him to gather and lead souls into his brothel, he will employ even worse men than themselves. But meanwhile they always remain Satan's brothel-keepers, and live off of that occupation. On this I leave you to consider how much the charity which they give can be pleasing to God. For He does not ever ask that charity be given from stolen goods, prostitution, or any wicked or dishonest gains, but instead He strongly condemns them just as He also vehemently condemned all dishonest gain, and particularly in those who are ministers in His Church (1 Tim. 3:8; Tit. 1:7). For this reason (as we already discussed previously on the seventh commandment) He forbids in His Law an offering taken from the wages of a harlot or a dog (Deut. 23:18). For if these reasons were acceptable, all thieves, usurers, brothel-keepers, harlots, and all others who accumulate wealth by iniquitous and dishonest occupations and means would be covered with the same cloak. For they could live at their ease by their profession under the guise of giving some portion of their profits to the poor, and under the guise of showing themselves a little more reasonable and fair and more kind in their occupation than others who might execute it worse than themselves.

Therefore it would be best for these ministers to faithfully do what they ought to do at the danger of being dismissed, and allow God to provide for the rest. For what can they judge of those who will succeed them? Perhaps at the end they will be found to be better men than themselves. If they do not desire to do what they ought to do, then let them refrain from mixing themselves up in the office in which they began. For, no matter how much they delude themselves in order to lull their consciences to sleep by excuses, yet they are assured that their excuses will not stand before the judgment of God, for which we must all prepare. Therefore it is not enough for us to satisfy ourselves or other men, for we must render an account to God, not to other men (Rom. 14:10; 1 Cor. 4:3-4).

Thus we must not make our consciences clear on our own accord, but we must measure them by the rule of the Word of God, and not by ourselves. For when all is said and done, if the men who set forth all these lovely excuses could hope to find such rich fare elsewhere as they have found here where they are, neither the edification nor the charity which they employ as their cover would delay them at all. I leave it to their consciences to judge, if they desire to recognize the truth without deluding themselves and continuing in lies any longer.

THOSE WHO HAVE RENOUNCED THE POSITIONS WHICH THEY CANNOT EXERCISE WITHOUT COMMITTING IDOLATRY, YET WHO STILL RECEIVE COMPENSATION FOR THEM, AND EXERCISE THE OFFICE VICARIOUSLY

TIMOTHY: I do not doubt that if these could be so well-off or live more at their ease somewhere else than they do where they currently make their residence, they would willingly forsake all. But what do you say of those who, having renounced such offices, give them to another person to exercise in their name, or under the title of resignation, and yet they nevertheless continue to receive the revenues and salary from it?

DANIEL: If they could find the means to have these goods in their own hands or to prevent the office from being filled (which cannot be done without blaspheming God), or to put it to better uses so that God would be honored and the poor members of Jesus Christ cared for, they would have some justification for what they do. But, seeing that God is always blasphemed by the people whom they have substituted for themselves in their place, I do not see that there is any great difference between these and the others we just spoke of, except that these are idolaters, thieves, and sacrilegious men vicariously, and the others are so in their own person. These are the hunters, and the men they put in their place are the decoys which assist them in their hunt. But we must pay attention to what is written: "Whoso is partner with a thief hateth his own soul" (Prov. 29:24).

THOSE WHO HAVE EMBRACED THE REFORMATION OF THE GOSPEL, AND WHO LIVE ON THE BENEFICES AND REVENUES OF THE CHURCH, BUT WHO DO NOT LABOR IN HER SERVICE

TIMOTHY: I am in agreement with you so far. But let us turn to others who are still among us who, having embraced the reformation of the Gospel, are left in the enjoyment of the benefices which they previously received in the papal church, on condition that they renounce all papacy and live according to the Word of God.

DANIEL: Seeing that the goods of the Church are dedicated to the preservation of her ministry and the care of her poor, it is quite certain that by right these goods must not be employed except toward the persons who are truly poor or those who are useful and necessary to the preservation of the Church and the ministry of the Gospel, without which she cannot be a church. Therefore those who have received a lifelong benefice, if they are not engaged in the ministry, must recognize that this is given to them as a special favor, and to support the infirmity which might be in them and in others like them, to entice them to the Gospel, and to remove from them any occasion that might hinder them. For by what right would this be due them if the rigor of the law were exercised rather than supporting them in equity and charity? Is it because they have been taken advantage of, and that they have taken advantage of others by leading them to perdition and dishonoring God? Must they have a reward for the evil they have done? As I do not wish to condemn the support which they use toward those by Christian love, in order that they are not left in despair, yet I would truly also like for them to understand that they cannot receive these revenues in good conscience unless they labor with all their power (according to the state to which God has called them) for the edification of the Church and the assistance of the poor, for which they receive these revenues.

TIMOTHY: Yet there are many of these who give very little consideration to the Word of God, but instead are more corrupt than any others, not only living in idleness without serving the Church or the public good at all except in scandals, but employing the revenues they receive from the church to support their games, harlots, and other wicked ways.

DANIEL: And this is how the revenues of the Church are put to good use!

YOUNG CHILDREN WHO RECEIVE A BENEFICE AND SALARY FROM THE CHURCH TO STUDY AND PREPARE THEMSELVES TO SERVE AS A MINISTER OF THE CHURCH, BUT WHO DO NOT FULFILL THEIR OFFICE

TIMOTHY: There are also young children to whom benefices are given beforehand on condition that they pursue their studies in order to serve in the ministry of the church, who however do the contrary, and follow the path of those of whom I just spoke. There are others who, though they have not previously received benefices in the papal church, yet their education is paid for out of the earnings of the Church for this same end. And then, when they have received their education at the Church's expense, they despise the office for which they were so hopefully educated, and prefer instead to apply themselves to other occupations and studies so that they can live more at their ease according to the world's standards. And, despite the fact that God has given them such good gifts to serve for the holy ministry, yet they bury in the earth the talents they received from Him.

DANIEL: You can easily judge with what conscience these people can enjoy the revenues of the church, and their relatives likewise, if they are the cause of their debauchery and if they have led them to it, as they often do, mocking both God and His Church after they have stolen from them for such a long time.

TIMOTHY: As for myself, I consider them genuine thieves.

CHAPTER SIXTEEN

Magistrates, Armies, and Theft

THE CONCERN WHICH RULERS MUST HAVE REGARDING THE DISTRIBUTION OF THE GOODS OF THE CHURCH, AND THE WEIGHTY CHARGE OF CONSCIENCE WHICH EXISTS IN THIS MATTER

DANIEL: It would be necessary for rulers and magistrates, who ought to be tutors and nursing fathers of the Church and its goods (Isa. 49:23), to consider these things in order to provide for and remedy them, seeing that this pertains to their office. For, seeing that they have taken the protection and charge of the administration of such goods, they must render an account of them to God, from whom they received this charge. Therefore, if there is error because of their fault, they will be required to give an answer to Him who gave them the protection of the Church.

For these goods are not for them, any more than the goods of orphans and wards belong to their guardians and protectors. Therefore if they squander them or allow them to be wasted, or if they dispose of them or distribute them in any way other than to the benefit of the Church and the uses to which they must be applied, they do not execute the office of good guardians and protectors, but rather that of plunderers, thieves, and sacrilegious men. For they must not consider it lawful as the guardian of the Church to do what is not lawful for other protectors and guardians to do, or even in the administration of the goods pertaining to the public domain, or even to our own personal goods. For, if we must all give an account of ourselves to God even for the wicked handling of the goods that He has given us personally, how much more will He require an account of us for our handling of the public goods and those belonging to the Church? (Rom. 14:12.)

THE SALE OF CHURCH GOODS; AND HOW THEY ARE LAWFUL OR UNLAWFUL, AND IN WHAT WAY

TIMOTHY: What you say is worth noting. What then should we say of those who sell and wholly dispose of these goods, not only as if they were their very own, but what is even worse, they sell them out of contempt and give them, in a manner of speaking, for a crust of bread (which they would never seek to do with their own personal property)? They do this out of covetousness for the gifts they will receive from those to whom they sell them, or for the favor they will receive from them.

What also must we say of these same who buy and sell the charity which has been left to the poor by legacies and wills?

DANIEL: I would not desire to condemn Christian rulers and magistrates or others likewise who have the management of the goods of another for the sale which they might make, if it were done not for the harm but for the benefit of the Church, the poor, the public good, and those to whom the goods belong, and if the money received were placed in more profitable purchases, as is done by Christian rulers. For a good guardian will work the best for the profit of the wards under his charge; indeed, each in his own personal goods. But if in making such sales the goods are wholly disposed of and lost by those to whom they belong by right, or if they are diminished to their harm, and those who sell them take as their own the money they receive from the sale, or only give the ward a paltry sum so that they might profit by taking the rest for themselves in order to spend it on their wine and their finery by the means you mentioned, I say that those who do such things are not only thieves, embezzlers, and workers of sacrilege, but true successors of Judas, who sell and deliver up Jesus Christ in His poor members—that is, in His Church and the public welfare, and the poor widows and orphans.

THE MAGISTRATES AND OFFICERS WHO TAKE TAXES, REVENUES, AND WAGES FROM THE PUBLIC PURSE, AND WHO DO NOT FULFILL THE OFFICE TO WHICH THEY ARE APPOINTED

TIMOTHY: Seeing that we have stumbled onto the topic of magistrates and public officers, what do you say, not only of those who become corrupted by bribes or who plunder and spoil the public goods under their charge, but also of those who, without parting with any of the salary assigned to them, never fulfill the charge for which they are being paid? Are they not also true thieves, just as the ministers of the Church who do not fulfill their office?

DANIEL: The reasoning is exactly the same. For why did God ordain taxes, income, tributes, and excises for rulers and magistrates (with which the poor people are charged), except for the salary of the office to which they are called and to maintain the expenses necessary for the administration of justice and the preservation of the public good?

Thus it is firstly required of them to acquit themselves of their duty and office by administering proper justice to every man without respect of persons.

Secondly, they must not ever sell justice for gifts or presents, but rather they must be content with their wages and in this way uphold the rule which John the Baptist gave to the soldiers who came to him to ask him how they ought to conduct themselves in their position, to which he responded: "Do violence to no man, neither accuse any falsely; and be content with your wages" (Luke 3:14).

SOLDIERS WHO ARE NOT CONTENT WITH THEIR WAGES AND WHO DO NOT FAITHFULLY SERVE THOSE FROM WHOM THEY RECEIVE THEIR WAGES

TIMOTHY: Seeing that we have come to the subject of soldiers, I believe that there is scarcely any type of theft of which the majority of them are not found guilty, seeing that there are very few, particularly of those who enlist of their own will, who scarcely go to the war for any other reason than the plunder they expect to find there. For, no matter how just the war might be, there are few indeed who content themselves with their wages and who, besides this, faithfully acquit themselves of their duty. (I do not here speak of those who pursue unjust wars, for I am reminded of what we discussed and considered under the sixth commandment concerning this matter. But I speak of those who serve in just wars and those who have the good cause on their side.) For, besides the thefts, plunders, and robberies they commit by stealing, pillaging, and ravishing all that they find unguarded, how much practice have they now received for stealing from the very rulers who set them to the task?

For, to begin, after the leaders and captains and all those who hold the highest ranks among the soldiers have received the money according to the companies they are required to muster, God knows how they distribute it and how they supply their companies. For, firstly, it very rarely happens that they fulfill their quota of men as they ought. For they have their stand-ins who stand in for their reviews, in which the captains go along with one another in their deception, or they borrow from other companies. In this way they steal all the money they receive above and beyond the number of soldiers they have.

Secondly, when it is a matter of assembling the soldiers, they do not worry about having the best they can get, except a small number who shine on the parade grounds and make the others look good. But they enlist many louts to fill up the ranks in order to pay them lower wages. For they bargain with them to see how much they will serve for, and whittle down their wages as much as they are able, taking the best deal they can get, just as butchers who buy meat.

Once again, by this they not only rob the soldiers, but also the ruler who pays them. They also place him in grave danger, for he believes he has a greater number and better men than he actually does. Yet he finds himself deceived, such that many kings and rulers and their kingdoms and people often fall into grave danger because of the lack of forces which they thought they had. And then it is very difficult for those men to employ themselves as they ought if they only go to war for the money. For, after they have it, they think of nothing except to gather their baggage and save their plunder.

But when I think about it, I'd truly be a fool to attempt to detail the various ways by which soldiers rob both rulers and people, seeing that war is like a license overflowing not only with all thefts, plundering, and ravishing, but also with all other wickedness.

DANIEL: To hear you speak, I'd think that you'd been engaged in the profession yourself. You truly understand their practices quite well.

TIMOTHY: I have experienced it more than I would care to do again. But I have not mentioned anything more than what is commonly known to all, even to little children and simpletons alike.

DANIEL: I have no doubt that those who practice this occupation could say much more, if they desired to declare what they know.

CHAPTER SEVENTEEN

Thefts Committed by Wives, Children, and Employees

THEFTS OF WIVES AGAINST THEIR HUSBANDS; AND OF CHILDREN AGAINST THEIR FATHERS AND MOTHERS

TIMOTHY: We have spoken of the highest positions and the grandest offices which exist among men. And, in speaking of wicked householders, you also declared in what way husbands and fathers of families could be thieves of their own possessions and those of their wives and children.

Thus I conclude by the same that wives and children can sin still more grievously when they are wicked managers, and when the wife plunders and steals the goods of her husband and squanders them, and when the children steal the goods of their fathers and mothers in order to spend them on vain and worthless things—that is, on their sensual pleasures, gaudiness, fine clothing, gluttony, drunkenness, debauchery, games, harlotry, and other such types of things.

DANIEL: Your conclusion is well founded. For if the husband and father of the family, who is the head, is rightly taken as a thief when he senselessly squanders the goods which he ought to preserve for his wife and children, with much greater reason we must consider as such the wife and children who, without the knowledge or will of the husband (or of the father and mother), take the goods of the house to use them according to their own pleasure, seeing that they are in subjection and that the lordship and government does not pertain to them at all, but to him whom

God has given as their head and governor. By this they sin not only against this commandment, but also against the one which God gave concerning the honor due to our father and mother and to our superiors (Eph. 6:1-3, 5-8). This is why it is written in Proverbs: "Whoso robbeth his father or his mother, and saith, It is no transgression; the same is the companion of a destroyer" (Prov. 28:24).

TIMOTHY: Yet there are few who trouble their consciences about this, for it seems to them that, because they are members of the household, they are not stealing goods belonging to another, but they are instead only using what is rightfully theirs.

DANIEL: But it is not in their power to do with it as they please, seeing that God has given them a governor by whose authority the goods must be dispensed. Otherwise, what confusion would exist in the house if the wife and children had no desire to acknowledge the master and ruler, but instead each one sought to reign according to his own desires? And if a wife is not faithful to her husband, nor the children to their fathers and mothers, to whom will they be?

This is about the same as if a man who was part of a community stole from the public purse, for he could allege that because he is a member of the community he did not take anything except what belonged to him. Yet he did not consider that, because these goods belong to others besides himself, he could not take them for his own personal use without theft, except by the will and consent of those who have a part in them, and particularly of those who are appointed governors over them.

THEFTS COMMITTED BY WASTEFUL WIVES AND CHILDREN, AND THE CARE AND INDUSTRY OF GOOD MANAGERS AND WISE CHILDREN

TIMOTHY: You spoke previously of extravagant men who destroy their wives and children by their wastefulness. But, if evil exists in this way on the side of the husbands and fathers, there is no less wickedness on the side of the wives and children when they are subject to this vice.

For, firstly, when the husband is wasteful and an evil manager of his affairs, if the wife is sober and a good manager of the household, there would still be a better order and more goods in the house than if she were wasteful or extravagant herself and given to finery, fashionable clothing, feasts, delicacies, and drunkenness, even if the husband were the best manager in the world.

DANIEL: This is seen by experience, for the wife's particular calling is to know how to economize and save. Therefore if she is wasteful, given to carnal pleasures, and subject to her own appetites, she is a bottomless abyss. But if she knows how to save, she could even keep and preserve many things to assist her in her management of the house at the proper time and place which her wasteful husband might depend upon.

TIMOTHY: I believe that you would not condemn such thefts committed either by the wives or the children, if they knew how to wisely keep and preserve what they see to be in danger of being foolishly squandered, in order to make it serve for the benefit of the household.

DANIEL: Such theft would not be theft, but rather prudence and wise management worthy of praise. But one theft greatly to be detested, and one which ought to engender great regret in the heart of wives and children, is when a wife's wastefulness, extravagance, and evil management drives her husband to beggary, to whom she was given as a helpmeet; and if the children force their parents to suffer need and to starve to death, whom they ought to provide for.

THEFTS OF SERVANTS TOWARD THEIR MASTERS AND LORDS

TIMOTHY: What you say is very true. Seeing that it is so, there is even greater reason to justly consider servants, maids, and all those who are in the service and employ of another, as thieves if they plunder or steal the goods of their lords and their masters and mistresses, or if they leave their goods to perish by their negligence, or if they do not serve them loyally as they ought.

DANIEL: You can clearly understand that if the father and mother of the family and the wife and children are to be condemned in this matter when they sin in this way with their own goods—which they have much greater right to than strangers—then we can easily judge those who have no right to them at all besides the charge of preserving and increasing the goods of another and receiving wages for their labor who are employed in this.

Secondly, if a man is a thief when he withholds the wages of the laborer whom he has hired, why wouldn't he also be one who receives wages not only for the labor which he ought to have done, but also for the harm he has caused his master? (Lev. 19:13.) And, as much as these have greater access and familiarity with those they serve, and as much as their employers trust them more than others, so much greater are they more execrable thieves than the others, and more dangerous, for they are both thieves and traitors at the same time. This is why Paul expressly admonished those who were in service not to be "purloining," or to become thieves and deceivers "unto their own masters" and their goods, but instead to serve them faithfully and labor the same in their absence as in their presence (Tit. 2:9-10). Therefore he exhorts them to serve "not with eyeservice" (Eph. 6:5-6; Col. 3:22). We can add to these servants all subjects who withhold the taxes or rights of their lords which they know is rightfully due them.

THEFTS OF LABORERS, TRADESMEN, AND WORKERS COMMITTED IN THEIR OCCUPATIONS AND PROFESSIONS; AND THE DANGER WHICH EXISTS ABOVE ALL IN MEN OF THE PEN, AND THE CONSIDERATION WHICH MUST BE TAKEN OF THEM

TIMOTHY: This teaching, in my opinion, extends to all laborers in general, and to all skilled workers, workingmen, and others like them who work for others, for these are all like public servants who truly desire to have a good salary from the work they do.

Therefore if they do not work faithfully in whatever profession they might choose, and if their labor is not worth the price they ask for it, they rob those who do business with them.

DANIEL: It is doubtless true. But the notaries, clerks, and writers are to be feared far beyond all others if they are dishonest, for they are the most dangerous. They hold in the power of their pen not only the possessions of men, but also their honor and their life. Therefore we can rightly say of them what Solomon said of the tongue, that "death and life are in its power" (Prov. 18:21). For, by a stroke of the pen, they can make a man lose his every possession, his honor, and his life. They can make him pay what he does not owe, and conceal what is owed to him. They can justify iniquity and condemn the innocent. In short, they are the ones who make the sentences of the judges, seeing that he must most often judge the possessions, body, honor, and life of men according to their writings.

Therefore it is greatly necessary to pay careful heed to which people are permitted into such offices, and to see that there is only a reasonable number of them. For, if the multitude of them is vast, it will be very difficult for all of them to live off of their profession without employing many wicked practices, and often employing themselves in creating wicked contracts. Yet there is today very little regard paid to this in many places, so much so that this profession is treated nearly the same as the state of the priesthood, which people choose for themselves because they desire to live more at their ease without laboring in any strenuous occupation.

THOSE WHO MAKE THEMSELVES COMPANIONS OF THIEVES BY DEALINGS WITH THEM

TIMOTHY: It seems to me that there is no great need for us to speak at any great length of the other professions in particular. For, in my opinion, we have sufficiently summarized them all in what we have already discussed among ourselves.

DANIEL: We can still add to those whom we have discussed all those who make themselves guilty of thefts committed by others, even though they did not commit them by their own hand except as much as they had dealings in some way with those by whom they were committed.

These dealings can be accomplished in numerous ways. Some have dealings with them by giving assistance or information to the thieves, or by furnishing them with the instruments necessary for their deeds. Others do so by commanding or inciting them to steal, and by giving them counsel or consenting to their theft, whether it is already committed or about to be committed. Others do so by permitting and not preventing the theft when they could have prevented it, or by not exposing it when they knew of it, or by concealing and hiding it themselves, or by participating in the plunder either by taking their own portion or by purchasing the goods from those who stole them. In short, no matter how we may be mixed up in it, we render ourselves guilty if we do not prevent it as much as we possibly can.

TIMOTHY: This agrees very well with the common proverb which says: "He sins as much who holds the bag as he who puts into it," and "He who accepts the hide is just as guilty as he who skinned the beast."

DANIEL: It is true.

GENERAL RULES GIVEN BY JESUS CHRIST AND HIS APOSTLES FOR THE KEEPING OF THIS COMMANDMENT

TIMOTHY: Seeing that we have amply spoken of both thieves and their companions, what do we have left to discuss?

DANIEL: To understand it all in general, we have no further need except to carefully note and to truly put into practice this law of Jesus Christ's which we already quoted when speaking of usurers, which says: "all things whatsoever ye would that men should do to you, do ye even so to them" (Mat. 7:12). And also what Paul sent to the Romans, saying: "Owe no man any thing, but to love one another" (Rom. 13:8).

We must also truly consider the fact that he admonished Christians to labor for the assistance of the poor instead of stealing, saying: "Let him that stole steal no more: but rather let him labour, working with his hands the thing which is good, that he may have to give to him that needeth" (Eph. 4:28). Paul here teaches us many things at the same time.

First, he shows that we must beware of doing any harm to our neighbor or of obtaining our profit by this means.

Second, instead of this we must obtain what we need by our own labor.

Third, whatever labor we may undertake is not unprofitable, no matter how difficult or arduous it might be, for it is indeed better for us to labor with our own hands, even if we can only do it in weakness, rather than flee labor to appropriate to ourselves the labor of our brethren by theft and by wicked practices and unlawful means.

Fourth, this labor only applies to lawful professions, occupations, trades, and honest employment worthy of a Christian man, as we have already said.

Fifth, we must not labor only for ourselves, but also for others who are in need.

TIMOTHY: This is a very good lesson.

DANIEL: We can also add to this same purpose what is likewise written to the Thessalonians: "[Let] no man go beyond and defraud his brother in any matter: because that the Lord is the avenger of all such" (1 Thess. 4:6).

In short, if we would consider that we are all created by the same God and the same Creator, and that we all bear the same image—which is His very own—we would recognize the bond of nature by which God has bound us to each other. This knowledge would induce us to a mutual love. This love would make us recognize how each of us are obligated to our brother, not only to do no harm to one another, but also to be of assistance and aid to all.

And if we also add "the bond of the Spirit of God" by which we are bound together in the same body and the same Spirit in Jesus Christ, we would be even more aware of the obligation we have toward one another (Rom. 12:4; 1 Cor. 12:13; Eph. 4:3). And, if we arrive at this understanding, not only will it keep us from sinning against this commandment, but also against all the others in the second table of the Law.

CHAPTER EIGHTEEN

Civil Punishments for Theft

CIVIL AND CRIMINAL PUNISHMENTS ORDAINED BY GOD AGAINST THIEVES, AND THEIR SUITABILITY WITH THE IMPERIAL LAWS

TIMOTHY: These are good rules, which contain and comprehend all. But what Paul adds of the vengeance of God on those who work harm and injury to their brother by their deceits and cunning reminds me that we have still not spoken of physical punishment and the vengeance which, according to the command of God, must be meted out against thieves (1 Thess. 4:6).

DANIEL: Though theft greatly displeases God, yet He did not command that all thieves ought to be put to death by the sentence of the judge. He ordained that restitution must be made by him who stole the beast of another, as it is written in Exodus. He did not only command that what the thief had taken must be restored, but that he must give many more beasts than one, according to the quality of the theft, as the Law declares (Ex. 22:1). We can apply this in general to all other thefts, just as Solomon declares in Proverbs (Prov. 6:30-31).

TIMOTHY: And if the thief is unable to offer satisfaction?

DANIEL: It is commanded that he be sold and placed in servitude in order to make repayment by his labor for the theft he committed.

Concerning those who break into and steal from houses

at night, if they are struck and killed, being caught in the act, the Lord gives pardon and delivers from all danger him who struck the blow. But if it happens during the day, He condemns to death as a murderer whoever kills the thief (Ex. 22:2-3). Concerning those who steal men, God has commanded what you already heard.

TIMOTHY: There is a greater similarity between these laws and the criminal punishments ordained by the imperial laws against thieves than the laws of our own day. For, as Justinian testifies, thieves were not condemned to death or sentenced to be quartered, but only to be flogged or banished, unless they were robbers who robbed someone by force either in the city or country, on the high sea, or on earth, or in public, for these were condemned to be hung. But now in our day all are hung, and particularly poor thieves and those who are the least guilty. But this is in repayment for the mercy shown to adulterers and harlots.

THE PUNISHMENTS AND VENGEANCE OF GOD AGAINST THOSE GUILTY OF SACRILEGE AND THOSE WHO ABUSE THE RICHES THEY HAVE RECEIVED FROM HIM

DANIEL: Chrysostom was not of the opinion that a theft which could be restored by restitution was worthy of death, but the severity of the law has now become much greater particularly against the poor, as you mentioned, who are no more than petty thieves who are often compelled to steal because of the wrongs or injuries done to them by strong and powerful thieves and robbers who escape the gallows much more easily than the others, or because they have for companions those who ought to be hung, or because they themselves take their place. But, though they escape the hand of man, they will not escape that of God.

Concerning workers of sacrilege, the example of Achan, who stained his hands in the plunder of Jericho, shows us how displeasing it is to God, and what vengeance He will bring against it (Josh. 7:1-26). We also have the example of Gehazi the servant of Elisha, who was struck with leprosy, along with all his descendants, because of his greed (2 Kings 5:20-27). And how dreadful must the example of Judas be to all those who daily sell Jesus Christ and His poor members?

Moreover, the example of Ananias and Sapphira and the two rich men who are mentioned in Luke's Gospel also amply shows us how all those who misuse the goods they have received from God will be treated by Him (Luke 12:16-21; 16:19-25; Acts 5:1-10). For, if Ananias and Sapphira were punished with such a horrible judgment for the hypocrisy they employed with their own possessions, feigning to give to the Church and the poor what they kept for themselves, what judgment must await those who, feigning to be guardians and preservers of the public goods and the goods of the Church and the poor, instead steal, pillage, and squander them rather than giving them to those to whom they belong?

We can say the same both of the rich man who was surprised by death at the very moment when he promised himself that he would enjoy the best of times in the midst of the vast abundance of possessions which he had, as well as the man who gave little thought to Lazarus the poor man full of sores, lying at his gate and begging alms (Luke 12:16-21; 16:19-25).

These men were not accused of pillaging or stealing the possessions of the poor, but only of not caring for them when they should have, and of misusing and squandering their riches on their own carnal pleasures and delicacies, and making them their gods. Therefore we must not doubt that a part of the great evils which daily come upon men by the providence of God, both in their bodies as well as in their souls and possessions, both by plagues and other diseases as well as by hail, storms, wars, looting, and other similar dangers and evils, are indeed sent from God to punish the various thefts daily committed by men who are not brought to justice and punished according to the commandment of God.

TIMOTHY: I agree with you wholeheartedly. We continually complain because of the wrongs and injuries done to us and our goods and the plundering and stealing which exists among men, and particularly among those who ought to be executing justice. But we must not doubt that we ourselves are the cause of it, and that God in this way punishes one sin by another, and one set of thieves by another set.

DANIEL: Now if God does not leave them unpunished even in this world by the means which please Him (though men do not give it much thought and may not perceive it), think what the judgment will be which awaits us after this life, in which "whatsoever a man soweth, that shall he also reap" (Gal. 6:7). For, if Jesus Christ so strongly rebuked those who despised Him in His members, what will He say to those who have stolen from and robbed them? (Mat. 25:45.)

Thus let us take careful heed to withdraw our heart so far from all greed that we never wrong anyone in the possessions which belong to them, nor even to ourselves, by misusing what we have received from God (Rom. 14:10; 1 Cor. 4:1-2; John 5:28-29).

TIMOTHY: May God give us the grace.

THE EXAMPLE OF ZACCHEUS CONCERNING THE LIBERALITY OF RICHES TOWARD THE POOR AND THE RESTITUTION OF THEFTS

DANIEL: Luke gives us two good points very worthy of being followed in the example of Zaccheus, who said to Jesus Christ: "Behold, Lord, the half of my goods I give to the poor; and if I have taken any thing from any man by false accusation, I restore him fourfold" (Luke 19:8). In the first place he does what Paul commands the rich to do: "that they do good, that they be rich in good works, ready to distribute, willing to communicate" (1 Tim. 6:18).

TIMOTHY: I think that this is the way in which Jesus Christ admonishes us to "make friends of the mammon of unrighteousness" and to "provide yourselves bags which wax not old" (Luke 16:9; 12:33).

DANIEL: It is true. The other point to note in this example is the restitution which Zaccheus made to those whom he had wronged. This is an action just as necessary, and we cannot boast of having truly repented of the thefts and wrongs we have done to our brothers unless we labor by all means possible to repay them if we have any way to do so.

For I cannot justly say that I have truly repented of my sin unless I am displeased with it. If I am displeased with the theft, I will no longer keep it with me, but will return what I have stolen to its owner. For if I am bound by the commandment which God gives me by Paul—to labor for those who are in need and to give them charity instead of stealing from them—how much more am I bound to return to my brother what I have taken from him and from his labor? I say this of those who are able to restore it. If the power and means to do so are lacking, they must cast it all upon the mercy of God.

THE TRUE RESTITUTION OF THEFTS, AND HOW IT MUST BE MADE, AND THE GREAT INIQUITY WHICH EXISTS IN THE CONFISCATION OF STOLEN THINGS WHEN THEIR OWNERS ARE KNOWN

TIMOTHY: From what I can understand from your words, it is not enough for a man who has stolen the possessions of another to simply donate them to charity if he does not also restore what he took to those from whom he stole it.

DANIEL: There can be no doubt of this. For God does not approve of charity given from stolen goods any more than He approves of stolen sacrifices, because He will not be made a companion of thieves.

TIMOTHY: What then do you say of the priests and monks who command men to give to the church what they have stolen, in order to make restitution for it?

DANIEL: They are companions of thieves.

TIMOTHY: And is it the same with those who make such

restitutions?

DANIEL: I consider them like Judas who, after having sold Jesus Christ, took the money he had received for betraying innocent blood and restored it to the priests at Jerusalem for restitution and satisfaction (Mat. 27:3-10). I see no great difference between them except that the money restored by Judas was better employed than the money given to these thieves and companions of thieves.

TIMOTHY: And if I have stolen from someone but it is impossible for me to restore it to him, what should I do?

DANIEL: Consider the poor, and provide for them.

TIMOTHY: Tell me also what you think of this custom which is received and approved of in another country: if a thief is caught by the law with his theft and then executed for it, the stolen possessions are confiscated by the ruler, even though the owners of the stolen goods are known and the owners themselves have assisted in the search for the thief.

DANIEL: It seems to me that this custom is the most iniquitous in the world, and contrary to all right and justice. In my opinion this is nearly the same as if a robber killed a thief and then seized what he had stolen and took it for his own. For justice was not established to take from men what belongs to them, but to see that it is restored to them, if the owners are known. If it is done otherwise, it is not justice, but highway robbery.

TIMOTHY: I agree with you perfectly. And, for the rest, I am content with all.

Made in the USA
Monee, IL
13 September 2026

62975592R00080